T0384662

The
TKT
Teaching Knowledge Test
Course

Young Learners Module

Kate Gregson

CAMBRIDGE
UNIVERSITY PRESS & ASSESSMENT

Shaftesbury Road, Cambridge CB2 8EA, United Kingdom

One Liberty Plaza, 20th Floor, New York, NY 10006, USA

477 Williamstown Road, Port Melbourne, VIC 3207, Australia

314–321, 3rd Floor, Plot 3, Splendor Forum, Jasola District Centre, New Delhi – 110025, India

103 Penang Road, #05–06/07, Visioncrest Commercial, Singapore 238467

Cambridge University Press & Assessment is a department of the University of Cambridge.

We share the University's mission to contribute to society through the pursuit of education, learning and research at the highest international levels of excellence.

www.cambridge.org
Information on this title: www.cambridge.org/9781009300766

First published 2024

20 19 18 17 16 15 14 13 12 11 10 9 8 7 6 5 4 3

Printed in Great Britain by Ashford Colour Ltd.

A catalogue record for this publication is available from the British Library

ISBN 978-1-009-30076-6 Paperback
ISBN 978-1-009-30078-0 eBook
ISBN 978-1-009-30079-7 Cambridge Core

Acknowledgements

First and foremost, thank you to the various teams at Cambridge University Press & Assessment: the Teacher Qualification team, in particular to Magnus Coney, who pored over initial drafts; Jo Timerick and Karen Momber for their continued help, support and dedication in seeing the writing project through to completion; and of course David Bunker, whose careful eye as editor helped improve both the quality of this book and my own thinking and writing. I'd also like to express my immense gratitude to Simon Smith, especially for his support with content, but also for all the help he has given me throughout much of my career. And finally, thank you to my husband, Richard Pearson, and our son James, whose patience with me was greatly appreciated.

Kate Gregson

The authors and publishers acknowledge the following sources of copyright material and are grateful for the permissions granted. While every effort has been made, it has not always been possible to identify the sources of all the material used, or to trace all copyright holders. If any omissions are brought to our notice, we will be happy to include the appropriate acknowledgements on reprinting and in the next update to the digital edition, as applicable.

Key: U = Unit.

Text

U2: Quote about learning strategies by Simon Smith. Copyright © Simon Smith. Reproduced with kind permission; **U3**: Text adapted from *Academy Stars Level 5 Pupil's Book Pack* by Steve Elsworth and Jim Rose. Copyright © 2017 Springer Nature. Reproduced with kind permission of the Springer Nature via PLSclear; **U4:** How to ask for help figure taken from *The 6 Principles for Exemplary Teaching of English Learners* by Joan Kang Shin, Vera Savic, Tomohisa Machida. Copyright © 2021 TESOL International Association. Reproduced with permission from TESOL International Association via CCC; **U5**: Text adapted from *Children Learning English* by Jayne Moon. Copyright © 2000 Macmillan Education Limited. Reproduced with kind permission of the Macmillan Education through CCC; **U9**: Text adapted from *Teaching Languages to Young Learners* by Lynne Cameron. Copyright © 2001 Cambridge University Press. Reproduced with kind permission of the Cambridge University Press through PLSclear; **Practice test:** Practice TKT YL test sourced from *Teaching Knowledge Test Young Learners*. Copyright © 2023 University of Cambridge Local Examinations Syndicate.

Photography

All the photographs are sourced from Getty Images.

U7: Liudmila Chernetska/iStock/Getty Images Plus; Lexi Claus/iStock/Getty Images Plus; **U8**: robertcicchetti/iStock/Getty Images Plus.

Illustrations

Practice test: Practice TKT YL test illustrations sourced from *Teaching Knowledge Test Young Learners*. Copyright © 2023 University of Cambridge Local Examinations Syndicate.

Typeset

Typesetting by QBS Learning.

Contents

Introduction

■ What are *TKT* and the *TKT: YL specialist module?*

The *Teaching Knowledge Test* (TKT) is a series of modular teaching qualifications which test knowledge in specific areas of English language teaching. It is internationally recognised and has been developed by Cambridge English. In addition to the main modules (Modules 1–3), there are the specialist modules, namely: *TKT: Young Learners* and *TKT: CLIL* (Content and Language Integrated Learning). Candidates can take as many TKT modules as they want, in any order and over any time period.

The *TKT: Young Learner Module* (TKT: YL) focuses on language learners aged 6–12; the term *young learner* is used in this book to refer to this age group. Six years old is usually the age when children start formal schooling in many countries, while twelve years old is around the end of primary, elementary or basic schooling. Developmentally, children in this age group are beyond the stage of early childhood, but are not yet adolescent. As such, they have particular developmental needs which are somewhat different from very young children or teenagers.

TKT: YL tests candidates' knowledge of concepts related to young learner learning and development, as well as knowledge of young learners from a teaching perspective: the planning, teaching and assessment of young learners' work. There are no entry requirements, such as previous language teaching experience or qualifications, however candidates' language skills should be at least at a B1 level on the CEFR scale. This is equivalent to Cambridge B1 Preliminary or Cambridge IELTS Bands 4–5, which is an intermediate level of English. Candidates are also expected to be familiar with key language teaching terminology, which can be found in the *TKT Glossary* on the Cambridge English website.

The TKT: YL test is a paper-based test lasting 1 hour and 20 minutes. It consists of objective tasks, for example matching or multiple choice, with 80 closed questions in total. Candidates respond by selecting answers and marking them on the answer sheet. There are no open response questions where candidates write their answers in words, phrases or sentences. Each question carries one mark, and performance is reported using four bands, which indicate the depth of the candidates' knowledge.

The test covers four syllabus areas, which are reflected in the four parts of this book, *The TKT Course: YL Module*:
1 Knowledge of young learners and principles of teaching English to young learners
2 Planning and preparing young learner lessons
3 Teaching young learners
4 Assessing young learner learning in the classroom

Note the *TKT: YL Module* is NOT a test of practical classroom skills or English language proficiency. The *TKT: YL syllabus* and other information about the test can be found in the *TKT: YL Handbook for Teachers*, which is available on the Cambridge English website.

■ About this book: *The TKT Course: Young Learners Module*

The TKT Course: Young Learners Module has five main aims:
1 To introduce readers to some of the main concepts, theories and activities that are central to TKT: YL and teaching language to young learners more generally.
2 To encourage readers to make links between theory and practice by analysing and exploring the usefulness of concepts, theories and activities in their own current or future teaching contexts.
3 To share with readers some of the resources available to teachers of young learners.
4 To give readers an opportunity to do test practice with TKT: YL sample tasks and a complete test paper (with answer keys).
5 To build on other TKT modules, for those who have done that course before doing The TKT Course: YL.

Who is *The TKT Course: YL Module* written for?

The TKT Course: YL Module is ideal for readers involved in teaching, who speak English as a first or additional language, and who:
• are training to become teachers or who are already teachers.
• are in a teacher, classroom assistant or course co-ordinator role.
• intend to take the TKT: YL test. They might be preparing for it on a course, with or without this as a core textbook, or preparing alone as self-directed learners.
• have done (an)other TKT module(s) and would like to continue their professional development in teaching young learners.
• are subject, generalist or language teachers of children aged 6–12.
• are already or are planning to teach English language to children aged 6–12.
• are already or are planning to teach English language in mainstream schools, private language schools or independently.
• are already or planning to be classroom assistants working with young English language learners aged 6–12.
• are undertaking in-service or pre-service training in teaching young learners.
• are young learner teacher trainers developing or delivering a TKT: YL test preparation course or other young learner teacher training courses. *The TKT Course: YL Module* may be used in its entirety or as a supplementary resource.
• are young learner course co-ordinators or teacher supervisors.

What is the content of *The TKT Course: Young Learners Module*?

The TKT Course: YL module consists of four parts, divided into units which follow the content and order of the TKT: YL syllabus and specifications. See the table on pages 4–5 for information on the organisation of each part.
The units build on each other so that the ideas introduced in one unit provide a foundation for ideas introduced in a following unit.

Part 1 focuses on knowledge of young learners and principles of teaching English to young learners.

Part 2 focuses on planning young learner lessons.
Part 3 focuses on teaching young learners.
Part 4 focuses on assessing young learner learning in the classroom.

The book also contains:

- A glossary of terms specific to teaching young learners which are used in the book. These occur throughout and are shown in **bold**.
  Terms in **bold italics** are those terms defined in the *TKT Glossary*, which can be found online.
  Other terms used are explained or defined as they first arise in the book.
- A complete TKT: YL practice test, answer key and sample answer sheet.
- Test tips for taking the TKT: YL test.
- An alphabetical list of the terms used in this book which are from the *TKT Glossary*.
- A glossary of young learner specialist terms and those which are included in the TKT: YL test.
- A list of titles referred to in-text and recommended further reading for each of the four parts of the book.

How is *The TKT Course: YL Module* organised, and how can it be used?

The advice in the following table is intended for those using the book on a taught course or for self-directed readers. The book can also be selected from or adapted for use by young learner teacher trainers.

The book is designed to help you, the reader, gain knowledge to prepare you for the TKT: YL test and also to support your professional development through insights gained from course content which you can apply in your own contexts. You are recommended to choose a young learner coursebook, supplementary materials and/or website to use for the activities found in each unit. Where possible, identify and keep in mind a specific learner, group of learners or teaching context for these activities. If you are not currently a practising young learner teacher, you could perhaps use another teacher's class of young learners.

You are strongly recommended to keep a *TKT: YL Professional Development (PD) Journal* as you use the book. In this PD Journal, you can keep notes and your responses to self-assessment, starter questions and activities, reflect on your learning from each unit, and consider how it might apply to your context. This could be in English or in your own language.

We hope you enjoy the challenge of teaching young learners, enjoy reflecting on your teaching of young learners and find yourself develop as a teacher of young learners. For those readers who take the TKT: YL test, all the best!

Each part of *The TKT Course: YL Module* follows the same structure:

Section	Purpose	Suggestions for use
Introduction to each part of the book	To encourage the reader to reflect on their current knowledge and experience in the broad topic area; to articulate their own learning objectives.	Do the self-assessment tasks before beginning this part of the book.
Three or four units, each with the same structure:		
Learning outcomes	To inform the reader of the knowledge and skills they should have after completing the unit.	Read these before you start the unit; add more if appropriate, based on your self-assessment.
Starter question(s)	To give the reader the opportunity to reflect on their understanding of the meaning of key terms or concepts before reading about these.	Answer the question(s) before reading the answer(s); you could use your TKT: YL PD Journal to note and organise your ideas and answers.
Key concepts	To introduce the main ideas of the unit content, drawing on the TKT: YL syllabus.	Read this after answering the *Key Concepts* pre-reading question. Build on your notes based on your reading.
Key concepts and the YL classroom	To consider how the key concepts influence or are relevant to young learner teaching and learning, specifically.	Read this after answering the *Key Concepts and the YL Classroom* pre-reading question. Build on your notes based on your reading.
Exploring the concepts in practice: Follow-up activity	To extend and deepen understanding of key concepts through active engagement. N.B. These questions do NOT follow the TKT: YL test question formats.	Do these tasks to extend your understanding on unit content, then check your answer in the commentary section towards the back of the book. You could use your TKT: YL PD Journal for this.
Exploring the concepts in practice: Reflection	To encourage the reader to think critically about questions and issues related to the key concepts in the unit.	Follow the guidelines for individual and/or group reflection tasks. You could use your TKT: YL PD Journal for this.
Exploring the concepts in practice: Discovery activity	To explore, investigate and develop key concepts in practice and assess their usefulness.	Follow the guidelines for these activities, which require exploration by reading, trying out new ideas, conducting classroom investigation and talking to others*.

	To review the unit content and to help readers become familiar with the TKT: YL task formats and level of language used in the text.	Do this task to familiarise yourself with the format of TKT: YL and to test yourself on the content of the unit. Recommended timing is built up to help you be ready for the test by the end of the book. Check your answers in the answer key on page 158.
TKT: YL practice task		
Reflection on learning in each part of the book		
Reflecting on Learning	To encourage the reader to self-assess their learning in this part of the book, identify any gaps in knowledge or understanding and articulate new learning goals, as necessary.	Follow the guidelines in this section for self-assessment and goal setting; you could use your TKT: YL PD Journal for this. Return to your self-assessment of the **can-do statements** in the unit introduction.
References and further recommended reading	To give ideas for extended, independent reading on topics covered in this part of the book. To list the sources referred to in this part of the book.	Note and follow up on sources which are useful to you for your own further development.

* Some activities recommend classroom investigation. In cases where data from or about children or other third parties, such as other teachers, is collected, **it is essential that ethical procedures are followed** in order to protect the rights of the participants. This will normally include gaining informed consent and/or assent from parents or caregivers before any data is collected for any purpose.

Part 1 | Knowledge of young learners and principles of teaching English to young learners

Introduction to Part 1

In Part 1, you will deepen your understanding of the characteristics of children aged 6–12 as learners, and consider the implications of this for teaching English to these learners. This part of *The TKT Course: Young Learner Module* will help you extend your knowledge and skills in preparation for the first part of the TKT: YL module test, namely, *Knowledge of young learners and principles of teaching English to young learners*. You can find more information in the TKT: YL syllabus in the module handbook, which is available online.

Specifically, in Unit 1, you will find out more about what makes young learners of English different from older learners, first by looking at the **developmental** benefits of learning English, and then by looking at ways we can enhance their language learning so that they can have these benefits. Finally, we look at classroom activities which are suitable for young learners, based on their characteristics.

Units 2, 3 and 4 will each introduce one of three kinds of strategy that children can develop through language learning: learning strategies, cognitive strategies and communication strategies. Each unit will explain what these strategies are, consider why they are important, and look at ways to develop and practise them in the English language classroom.

Each unit also includes suggested reader activities for extension, reflection and investigation into your practice. These activities will help you consolidate your understanding and relate your learning to your own classroom *context*. A range of activities are suggested in each unit, and you can find a sample TKT: YL practice test section on the unit topic at the end of each one. You could use your TKT: YL PD Journal to keep your notes and reflections for the questions and activities organised.

Before you begin, look at the *can-do statements*. Evaluate your own understanding and skills for each one. After completing Part 1, return to these and re-assess yourself. From that, you can develop an action plan so that you can continue to focus on any particular areas you feel you still need or want to develop.

SELF-ASSESSMENT

	Rate yourself from: 1 (*Limited or not at all*) to 5 (*This is a strength*)	Rating before Part 1	Rating after Part 1
1	*I can* talk about some characteristics of 6–12-year-old children as language learners.		
2	*I can* identify and justify a range of language learning activities which help children develop learning strategies.		
3	*I can* identify and justify a range of language learning activities which help children develop cognitive strategies.		
4	*I can* identify and justify a range of language learning activities which help children develop communication strategies.		

In your TKT: YL PD Journal, identify two or three questions or areas you'd like to know more about in each unit in Part 1. When you have finished Part 1, return to these to see if you have answered them. If you haven't, read around the topic using the recommended reading list at the end of Part 1. You can also find CPD advice on the Cambridge English website, and many more resources for teacher professional development online.

Unit 1 Children as language learners: What are the characteristics of children as language learners?

LEARNING OUTCOMES

By the end of this unit, you will…
KNOWLEDGE: know about some characteristics children bring to language learning
SKILLS: be able to make connections between activity types and the benefits they bring to the young learner classroom

■ Starter Question

Before you begin this unit, read the starter question and make some notes. Then read the commentary and compare it to your notes.

 Why do we teach English to 6–12-year-old children? **Note at least three points.**

COMMENTARY

Nowadays, children around the world are beginning to learn English from an ever younger age at school and outside of school (**extracurricular**). This is partly because of a popular belief that starting earlier with English will give children greater linguistic benefit than starting later, so it will allow them to finish school with a higher level of English, ready for their futures as young adults. However, research shows that older learners usually make faster progress and learn more efficiently as they are cognitively more mature, have better learning skills and are more skilled at interaction and communication (see Read, 2003 for a more detailed discussion on this).

Despite this, there are plenty of benefits in other areas to an earlier start. 6–12-year-old children are still developing cognitively, physically, socially and emotionally, as learners, as individuals, and as thinkers; learning English can play a part in this development. Classroom learning at **primary** level, usually from around 5 or 6 until 10 to 12 years old, is often based around fun and engaging activities which help children develop in different areas, and English language learning also lends itself to these kinds of activities more than to formal desk-based learning. If positive learning conditions are established through such activities, then it is likely that learning English as a foreign language may help children develop positive *attitudes* and improved *motivation* for English in preparation for **secondary** school. Learning English can also help them to develop personal and educational skills as well as the '4 Cs': *Communication, Collaboration, Critical thinking* and *Creativity*, which are important to their all-round development and being ready for the 21st-century world.

Attitudinal benefits

If children receive positive experiences of learning English in primary school, this will help them to develop self-esteem as well as a positive *attitude* towards English, other English speakers and learners, and to their own abilities as learners. Even in a society which uses little English, many children also encounter English outside of the classroom, such as on the TV or in songs, and for some older primary children, in video games or on social media. These learning opportunities can be highlighted and exploited for learning in school to help children develop a positive attitude. All this lays the foundation for the confidence and skills needed for the more formal learning of English which typically happens in secondary school.

Social benefits

Children can learn skills to socialise from communicating and collaborating with other children in *pairs*, in groups and as a *whole class*, as well as in communication with their teacher. They may learn, for example, to take turns in a guessing game, to listen to a classmate's idea without interrupting or to ask the teacher a question if they don't understand an instruction; children can also learn to collaborate by contributing individually to a group task.

Intercultural benefits

Children can learn to understand their own culture as well as other cultures and people through learning English. Classroom activities involving songs and stories from their own and other countries, for example, can help them see similarities and differences between known and unfamiliar cultures. Intercultural projects, for example *eTwinning*, or email exchange projects with children in other countries can also provide excellent opportunities for children to develop intercultural understanding, tolerance and global awareness while using English for real communication with other learners, which is an authentic use of language.

Cognitive benefits

Children aged 6 to 12 are also developing as thinkers, and some may still be learning to carry out such mental tasks as classifying, sequencing, and hypothesising. Language learning activities involving **puzzles**, questions or **games**, and *open questions* from the teacher will enable them to develop their critical thinking skills.

Learning to learn benefits

Children can develop strategies such as *predicting* the content of a story from looking at pictures or a book's cover, planning work when doing a group project, reviewing and evaluating their learning at the end of a *coursebook* unit. These are known as *learning strategies*. Learning English, then, can help children to learn educational skills which are important in all **school subjects** and in their life outside school.

Physical development benefits

Children aged between 6 and 12 are still developing physically. Younger children are still developing **fine motor skills** such as cutting and folding paper and are also learning to coordinate their hands and eyes so that they can do such things as write on lines, colour in pictures neatly and use space on the page when they make drawings. This means that language learning activities which require children to make or draw things may have a value in the child's overall development, which adds to the benefit they gain from learning language. Such activities also help children's creativity, as can other design activities, creating stories, characters, funny animals and so on.

Academic benefits

Children can extend or consolidate learning in other school subjects through English. This combination of English and subject-related learning is known as *CLIL* (Content and Language Integrated Learning). English may be used as a **language of instruction** in schools, or learning might be extra-curricular, that is in addition to what children learn in school: for example, they may find out about different animal habitats through a *communicative* activity in an English language lesson which they haven't learned about in their science lessons at school.

■ Key concepts

> Reflect on the *key concept* question. Brainstorm your ideas, then expand your notes as you read.
>
> *What are some similarities and differences in teaching children of various ages?* **Note one or two of each.**

COMMENTARY

There is a big difference between teaching English to a class of 6- and 7-year-olds and to a class of 11- and 12-year-old children, and these differences are generally greater than we would find in a similar age range difference in adults. In comparison to 6- and 7- year-olds, for example, children aged 11–12 are likely to have more developed *literacy* skills and a more mature first language system. They are often better able to control their emotions, can sometimes explain their thoughts about learning and language and have more experience and knowledge of the world in general. However, characteristics often depend more on the individual child than their age because all children learn and develop in different ways and at different speeds.

Even though there is a difference within the age group, there are plenty of common characteristics which, in turn, distinguish the 6 to 12 age group from older children or adults as learners of English:

A capacity for play and fun

Language and skills practice can be transformed into **game-like activities** which will let children satisfy this capacity. We can review vocabulary and practise speaking by playing *charades* or drawing games (such as *Pictionary*-like games), or mime actions while listening to an **action song,** for example. Children may also be engaged by online or app-based games for language learning, some of which are specifically designed for children learning English, for example, *Ruby Rei* by Cambridge English/ Wibbu. Halliwell (1992, p. 6–7) gives an example of children making an activity game-like: a class of 9- and 10-year-olds were following directions on a map in order to check whether statements the teacher made about the shops on the map were true or false. One pair of children had a paper clip and pretended to 'drive' it around the map in response to the teacher's directions. They made car and brake noises as they 'drove' their paper clip. This example illustrates children's ability to use their imagination, and the pleasure many of them take in physical activity.

A capacity for indirect learning

Although some children at the upper end of the 6–12 age spectrum are able to analyse language as a system, many younger children may have limited abilities to do this. On the other hand, most younger children will respond very well to motivating activities which give them a chance to experience and use the language. Their motivation is likely to come less from the concept of language as a system, and more from the idea of language they can use to have an enjoyable experience such as singing a song, saying a *chant*, or playing a game. Children are more likely to understand and remember language if it involves tasks and situations like these, which seem familiar in their world, as they provide a motivating and memorable context for the foreign language. As an example, children may enjoy and experience a game in which they guess where the class puppet has hidden a toy. It is of course a guessing game, but the teacher may also be using it to practise *yes/no* questions. In other words, language is the vehicle of classroom learning, not the driver.

An ability to make sense of language

When children learn their first language, they don't understand all the words that people around them say to them. They rely on **intonation, gestures, facial expressions** and other clues in the situation they are in to understand the different messages they hear, and from this making sense, they are able to learn the language itself.

When children start to learn a foreign language at school, they can be encouraged to use these same skills involved in interpreting the general message in order to make sense. This is partly because many children at the beginning of primary education may be starting to read and write English at the same time as they are learning to read and write their own language, which means they are not able to support their learning by reading or writing. This is particularly true if children's **first language** has a different script from English.

An ability to learn from interacting with others

Many young children, therefore, learn well from talking and listening to peers and to the teacher, as listening and speaking are the main channels they use to make sense in their world. Pair work, group work and shared whole-class activities provide a platform for children to learn both concepts and language from each other and the teacher. They can also help children develop social skills of interaction.

An ability to use limited language creatively to communicate

Consider the child who is talking about what they find in the kitchen. This child says, 'a hotter', referring to the cooker, because she had recently learned the word 'hot', but didn't know the word 'cooker' or 'oven'. This example shows how the child was using their mental and linguistic resources imaginatively in order to communicate the meaning of an unknown word. It also demonstrates the child's willingness to experiment and take risks with language in order to express their own meaning. Board games and other similar games, such as the word game *Taboo*, can help children in this way: the player has to explain a given word without using certain other words (which are commonly associated with the word to be guessed).

*An ability to use **chunks** to communicate*

Children may be able to use complete phrases such as *It's my turn*, *Don't do that!* or *See you later!* in the correct situations even though they haven't been taught them formally. Such phrases are called ***chunks***, and are examples of language children have learned as whole phrases by picking them up from other people. This is a very different characteristic from the ability to experiment with language to create meaning, and also typical of young learners of a foreign language. Chunks are particularly useful because they help children to join in conversations or to meet a need in the English-speaking classroom and because children can often use them to create new phrases. If a child has learned *Can I go to the toilet?*, for example, they can use part of the chunk in other phrases such as *Can I turn on my microphone?* or *Can I get my pencil case?*.

A need to feel valued, relaxed and safe

Children are not very different from adults in this respect. However, children are still developing socially and emotionally as people, so they respond especially well to environments where they feel confident enough to contribute without fear of being laughed at or criticised by others. Some children may not say very much because they don't feel comfortable speaking English when they first begin learning, a phenomenon known as 'the Silent Period'. Avoiding pressure to speak until ready, and providing plenty of ***receptive*** skill activities (e.g. listening) where learners are not required to speak before having children use ***productive*** skills (e.g. speaking) is recommended. We can help children feel valued in the classroom by giving them responsibilities, such as cleaning the board, shutting down the computer, collecting or distributing materials. Listening and giving feedback on each learner's efforts also helps them feel a part of the class. This all further helps their confidence as well as develops them emotionally.

Characteristics which vary among children

Every child is unique. We saw above that children develop in different ways and at different rates, and each child brings their own personality and experience to the classroom. Added to this, individuals have different ***learning preferences***, for example they may find they remember words better when they see a picture or when they hear a word in different contexts. Some children will enjoy singing or dancing to English songs, while others may prefer to work quietly on their own or with a friend; younger children often have shorter ***attention spans***, and need to move around or change activities frequently, much more than older children or adults, although this will again vary among children. While these differences are the same in adult and older learners, young learners may vary more widely and become disengaged in something that does not suit them. So, we should include a wide variety of different activity types in our lessons and try to notice how well our learners respond to different activities.

■ Key concepts and the YL classroom

> **Reflect on the *key concepts and the YL classroom* question. Brainstorm your ideas, then expand your notes as you read.**
>
> *What kinds of classroom activity might be suitable for young learners, based on their characteristics?*

COMMENTARY

When teachers teach young learners aged 6 to 12, we need to keep the characteristics we have identified in mind. We can do this by planning for different kinds of classroom activity so that we can support different children at their stage and pace of development and learning. The following principles are useful to keep in mind:

- We can motivate children by stimulating their creativity, imagination, physical and cognitive development through activities such as *visualisation*, art and *craft* activities and other creative tasks which play with language. Using and creating *props*, *flashcards*, pictures, video and digital media can also support learning.

- We can use various *interaction patterns* such as pair work, group work and individual work, helping children learn to work in these ways by giving particular roles for group work, and clear guidance on behaviour.

- We can make connections between children's home and their school by involving and communicating with parents/caregivers, having children bring things from home and using familiar activity and material types such as **picture books**, songs and familiar games.

- We can manage children's energy and attention by planning for lots of short activities (increasing in length as children get older), varying the lesson pace and intensity, following a pattern of *stir* (active, higher energy activities) then *settle* (calmer, quieter activities), stir then settle, stir then settle and so on.

- We can also bring plenty of physical movement into our lessons to help manage energy further, for example using *Total Physical Response* (TPR) activities. TPR is a language teaching method which involves children responding in a physical way to orders or instructions the teacher gives (e.g. *Point to the window; Jump three times*). As children's comprehension and confidence develops, the teacher can build longer chains of instructions or more complex instructions for children to follow, and children can also start to give their own instructions for their classmates to follow. TPR builds on children's ability to make sense of language *input*, responds to their need for physical movement, exposes them to understandable and useful *chunks* of language and can appeal to their sense of play and fun, especially if the orders are humorous. TPR can also support children's need to feel relaxed and safe, as they are not forced to speak until they feel confident enough to do so.

- We can set up *routines* for any stage of the lesson, although commonly at the beginning and end of a lesson. Routine actions are those we do regularly (e.g. daily routine), while routines in the classroom are activities or interactions which are repeated at the same point or for the same purpose in a lesson. They can help *classroom management* during **transitions** or particular activity types (e.g. moving to **circle time**). For example, a routine might be when we use a particular song or exchange as a greeting at the start or end of a lesson, to organise the giving out and collecting of materials for a lesson, for children to make pairs, or to quickly stop a groupwork activity. Routines are important because their familiarity can help children to feel relaxed, safe and confident. They also provide important opportunities for children to make sense of meaning, to interact and to learn language (see Cameron, 2001, for more on routines). Routines can also support social and emotional development by encouraging good social behaviour, such as when the teacher asks children to tidy up at the end of an art and craft activity.

■ Exploring the concepts in practice

FOLLOW-UP ACTIVITY *(see page 149 for answers)*

Read about the series of classroom activities shown in part of a lesson outline and answer the question.

Lesson outline extract

Teacher action	Student action
Ask students to mime what they do in the morning before school	Mime some daily morning routine actions
Play the YouTube video animated story about daily routines	Mime the daily routine actions
Review/introduce target language and set up pairwork activity	Practise target language: 'What time do you...?'
Set up short group survey activity	In groups, plan and conduct short survey to find out about friends' daily morning routine
Set **at-home task**	At home, survey family or friends about their daily morning routine
NEXT LESSON Show example of table and model how to make a table on the computer; provide technical help	Create a table on the computer to present their findings; print it and stick to notice boards
Model and participate in **gallery walk**	Walk around, ask questions and talk about each other's tables

Question:
Which of the following statements are true and which are false? Explain your answers.
A The activities help children use and develop physical, cognitive and social skills.
B Children work individually, in pairs and as a group in these activities.
C Children hear the *target language* (daily routine vocabulary and question-answers) before they have to say it.
D Children use chunks of language.
E This is a classroom routine.
F There are possible home-school connections in these activities.
G These activities are only suitable for children in the younger age range.

REFLECTION

**Arrange to meet other teachers in your institution, school or context, if possible. Alternatively, you could meet online or do this task in an online group or forum with teachers in another context.
Do the task together.**

1 How would you explain young learner characteristics as learners of English to a teacher who has not taught children before?

2 How do you provide opportunities for children to use their imaginations in your own teaching?

3 Which routines do you use in your own teaching and why?

DISCOVERY ACTIVITY

> **Look at the three discovery activities to explore teaching and learning in your context. Choose and do at least two which are most useful for you in your context.**

1 Think about a lesson you taught recently and/or ask a colleague to describe a lesson they taught. How did the lesson support learners' development in different ways (e.g. cognitive, social, emotional, physical and linguistic)?

2 Choose an activity in a young learner coursebook or resource pack. Identify at least one non-linguistic benefit it may have for your learners.

3 Think about the chunk *Can you...?* How could you use TPR in an activity to give learners the opportunity to practise this chunk?

■ TKT: YL Practice task

> **Do the practice task for this unit. Time yourself to see how long you take to answer all the questions.**
> **Then check your answers in the answer key on page 158.**

For questions **1–6**, match the teacher's comments from self-observation about their English lessons with the characteristics listed **A–G**.

There is one extra option which you do not need to use.

Children's characteristics

A A love for physical movement	**E** Pleasure in using their imagination
B An ability to use language chunks	**F** A love for practical responsibilities
C An inquisitive nature	**G** A love for routines
D Different learning preferences	

Teacher's comments

1 '...The children were really engaged when I told them about my cat. They were fascinated and asked lots of questions about my cat!...'

2 '...The children had plenty of great ideas when I asked them to guess the ending to the fairy story....'

3 '...There is always a lot of laughter when learners mime and gesture as they listen....'

4 '...My learners are very keen to help me in the classroom – so many of them raise their hands to offer to check the computer is shut down at the end of the class....'

5 '...As usual, learners told me three words they remembered from the lesson before they left the classroom....'

6 '...In the lesson, I planned some activities where learners worked individually because many learners work well individually....'

Unit 2 Developing children's learning strategies: How can I help children develop their learning strategies through language learning?

LEARNING OUTCOMES

By the end of this unit, you will…
KNOWLEDGE: know more about the benefits of learning strategies to children's language learning
SKILLS: be able to identify a range of learning strategies and ways of helping children to develop them through language learning

■ Starter Question

Before you begin this unit, read the starter question and make some notes. Then read the commentary and compare it to your notes.

 Why do you think it is useful to help children develop strategies which help them learn? **Note two or three reasons.**

COMMENTARY

Learning strategies are techniques children use to help them learn, and in this case, learn English specifically. They may use some techniques consciously, and some unconsciously. Learning strategies are useful to children because they help them to become more autonomous, independent learners as they develop greater understanding of what learning is and, therefore, how to learn without as much help from the teacher. Through this, they improve their ability to learn. Children can also apply many learning strategies they use for English to other **subjects** in the *curriculum*; they may already use learning strategies to help them learn in other subjects which they can transfer to learning English.

Teachers can teach children learning strategies explicitly, and can ask them to practise them at home and in class. They can also highlight the connections between English and other subjects in the curriculum, which will further motivate children in their learning of English. Teachers will benefit from having more confident and efficient learners in class, and they will be able to see how different children in their classes learn best. From here, the teacher can plan and manage learning better for the specific groups of children they teach.

■ Key concepts

> Reflect on the *key concept* question. Brainstorm your ideas, then expand your notes as you read.
>
> *What can we focus children's attention on to help them become better learners?* **Give one or two examples.**

COMMENTARY

Learning is an active process, undertaken by the learner, and we can help children become better language learners and learners in life in general by helping them become more expert in the skills needed for the learning process. This may involve helping children to understand about learning (metacognitively), be ready and willing to learn better (emotionally) and develop the skills which will help them learn better (learning strategies). Ellis and Ibrahim (2015, p. 9) explain that:

> Learning to learn is primarily concerned with the *processes* of learning, and aims to focus the child's attention on what they are doing – and why – in order to develop their awareness of the learning process and better understand *how* they learn, in addition to *what* they learn.

Understanding about learning

Metacognition is defined by the Cambridge online Dictionary as 'knowledge and understanding of your own thinking', in this case knowledge and understanding of the learning process. Being more aware of how people learn languages can undoubtedly help children learn more efficiently, so by making this process explicit to learners, we can support them in their English language learning. This may include the teacher explaining to learners why they are doing an activity in the classroom, or how an **at-home** or out-of-class activity will support their English learning. Helping children learn to plan, track and evaluate their learning is also metacognitive.

Being ready and willing to keep learning

An important factor in learning is **motivation** for learning, as motivation will encourage a child to keep learning. There are many aspects to motivation: A teacher might motivate children to learn through providing engaging activities, interesting content and being sensitive to children's needs in the classroom, for example. We can also help children to develop intrinsic motivation – the motivation which comes from within – and a love for learning in general by encouraging a growth mindset, which helps children see that everyone can reach a learning *goal* if we take it step by step (Dweck, 2006). In this way, an intrinsically motivated learner will continue learning by reaching smaller learning goals, one by one. Through showing learners how they are progressing and praising and rewarding effort, for example, children will be encouraged, be motivated and will want to keep learning more and more.

Being supported as an individual

Each child develops and learns in their own way and at their own rate. This can depend on various influential factors, such as the social and learning context, the topics and activities, the teacher, the learner's personality and their mood. Keeping notes on how different children use particular learning strategies can help the teacher understand and take each learner into account in their teaching, and therefore value diversity in their classroom.

■ Key concepts and the YL classroom

Reflect on the *Key concepts and the YL classroom* question. Brainstorm your ideas, then expand your notes as you read.

 What learning strategies do/could you use with children in your classroom? **Note at least three strategies.**

COMMENTARY

The teacher may implement different strategies in the classroom to help children understand the learning process and become more motivated to learn. These include the following:

Learning strategy	Example
Planning learning	Before drawing a picture of rooms in a house and writing a short description of it, two children agree on who will draw, who will write, and on how long they will take for each task.
Setting learning *objectives*	In a tutorial at the beginning of the school year, a child tells the teacher that this term she wants to learn ten words about sports.
Selecting activities	For a **project** on animals, the teacher asks children to work in groups. She lets each group choose whether to create a quiz or design a poster.
Organising learning	A learner writes new words she has learned from a **graded reader** under the headings of *Clothes* and *Colours*.
Reviewing learning	A child looks through a coursebook unit their class has just finished and thinks about what they have learned.
Remembering language	A child looks at a new word, says it to himself, covers it, writes it down, and then checks that his spelling is correct.
Using **reference resources**	A learner isn't sure about the meaning of a word he reads in the coursebook. He uses the glossary in the coursebook to check its meaning.
Developing hypotheses about language rules	As a result of hearing the teacher using *he* and *she* in class, and in an animated song video, a child develops an idea that *he* is used for men or boys, and *she* for women or girls.
Comparing	As a child listens to a song from the coursebook, she listens for similarities in vocabulary between English and her **L1**.
Contrasting	While watching a coursebook video clip on the topic of families, a child notices that English has just one word for *aunt* and *uncle*. He finds this interesting, because in his language there are many different words.
Self-assessment	A child reflects after performing a dialogue with a classmate to the rest of the class. She thinks that her pronunciation was good because she said the words quite clearly but decides that she should speak more loudly next time because sometimes her partner needed to ask her to say something again.
Self-correction	Learner: (looking at a picture of a street scene) *I can see two mans.* Teacher: *OK, but... two mans?* Learner: *Men... I can see two men.*

Teachers can help children to develop learning strategies through using a *Plan → Do → Review* model in class. The three stages of the *Plan → Do → Review* model simply involve, first of all, children thinking before an activity about what they already know, and what they need to prepare or consider in order to do an activity successfully (Plan). Children then do the activity (Do), and after it review and assess what they did well, and what they could do better next time (Review). Cycles of *Plan → Do → Review* can be integrated into normal teaching practice easily, as it is a very similar classroom approach to using activities *before, while* and *after* when children are focusing on listening, speaking, reading or writing.

The **KWL model** can also support learning strategies. In this model, before a topic, lesson or classroom activity, children **brainstorm** what they already **K**now (content and/or language). Then they express what they **W**ant to know, that is they set learning objectives, also in relation to content and/or language. Once the topic, lesson or activity is over, they return to their objectives, reflect and say what they feel they **L**earned. This can be extended for older children to include planning how they might learn something (at the *Know* stage) and by identifying questions they still have at the *Learned* stage, including how they will go about answering these questions (i.e. goal setting). This can be done individually or in **pairs** or groups, using a **KWL chart**. Examples of these are widely available online.

In addition, teachers can help children to develop effective learning strategies by explaining specific examples to them, by providing opportunities for children to think about their learning individually, and by giving them chances to explain and share strategies they use for learning to their classmates.

Explaining learning strategies to children

Here is an example from a young learner *coursebook*. This page starts the coursebook unit. The Teacher's Guide recommends teachers draw attention to the unit learning *objectives* listed at the top of the page; learners then share and discuss their opinions and brainstorm content-related knowledge before the unit starts by answering the questions on the first page, as shown. At the end of the unit, the teacher will return to these to help children evaluate their learning.

Extract from Zapiain (2020) *Cambridge Primary Path* Student's Book 2: Cambridge University Press & Assessment

The teacher may decide to explain to her class why this activity supports their learning, and can ask children to reflect on this strategy. If the coursebook does not include a focus on learning strategies, teachers can suggest strategies themselves for children to try out, reflect on and talk about together in class.

Providing opportunities for children to think about their work individually
As younger children's abilities to select appropriate learning strategies and analyse and explain their thoughts are often less developed than those of older children, teachers can ask younger children to provide simple visual responses to learning, for example by asking them to put their thumbs up, sideways or down, or to indicate with smiley faces or other symbols (e.g. ♥ ♥ ♥) how much they enjoyed an activity or how well they think they did. They could also complete a termly or unit checklist of **can-do statements** or lesson objectives, which children tick off as they achieve them.

It's important also to go beyond visual responses to get children to think a little more deeply and to consider the reasons why they enjoyed activities; any discussion of this, both for younger and older children can be in L1 if necessary, as the main focus is not on practising language, but on developing learning strategies. Older children will respond more readily to linguistic prompts, and so teachers can find out about learners' learning and their own teaching through oral or written questions such as *What did we learn today? What was useful and why? What did I do well? What can I do better next time?* This learner self-assessment can also give the teacher an impression of the learners' learning so they can make changes to their teaching if necessary.

Giving children opportunities to share and explain their learning strategies
Before starting an activity, teachers can encourage children to think about possible learning strategies they can use to be successful. For example, if children are going to design a group poster about healthy food, teachers may ask children how they will use their time so that they work effectively. Children's responses (e.g. *agree what food to include, agree a format for presenting, do a draft version first, agree who does what, allow time to review what we've done*) can be shared in **plenary**, that is as a **whole class**, giving children a chance to learn from each other and try out new strategies. The responses also provide teachers with a chance to highlight effective strategies and to find out important information about children's **attitudes** and skills in learning.

After an activity, children can also share learning strategies they used. For example, after an at-home task which involved children saying and remembering some questions, children can compare how they practised in the next class (e.g. *I looked, said out loud, covered, said again, practised with someone at home, cut each question into separate words and reassembled them.*).

Out-of-class learning strategies
We can encourage learners to find English in their home or local environment, which will help them become more independent, autonomous learners. An at-home activity could be to find and play a word game on a mobile phone or other device, to watch a cartoon in English (with or without subtitles in English or their own language), to find some English print in their local environment (e.g. signposts, food packaging etc.) or to find an English song they like and learn some words or lines from it. Requesting parent/caregiver support will also open up an additional learning strategy; even if their English proficiency is limited, they could partner their child in their language learning journey.

■ Exploring the concepts in practice

 FOLLOW-UP ACTIVITY *(see page 149 for answers)*

	Read the teachers' questions and choose an appropriate response for each. Then do the tasks.

Teachers' questions	Possible responses
Teacher 1: How can I deal with parents or caregivers who think that focusing on learning strategies isn't very useful for their children?	A Adapt or **supplement** your materials by including a focus on learning strategies from time to time.
Teacher 2: How can I encourage a growth mindset among my learners?	B You can help them see that we learn little by little. Praise each learner's efforts at each step of learning, however big or small – that sized step is for that learner. Then show them where to go next and how to get there.
Teacher 3: What can I do if my coursebook or **syllabus** doesn't provide opportunities for children to think about learning strategies?	C You can integrate the Plan – Do – Review model into your normal classroom teaching, with Planning occurring at the pre-lesson or task stage and Reviewing at the post-lesson or task stage.
Teacher 4: How can I help children **in mixed level** or **mixed ability** classes focus on learning strategies?	D You can write a letter to them explaining why you are focusing on learning strategies. You can also invite them to come and talk to you if they are still worried.
Teacher 5: How can I include development of learning strategies into my already full class time?	E You can highlight the learning objectives at the beginning of the lesson. At the end of the lesson, you can ask learners to show you thumbs up, thumbs down or thumbs sideways, in response to your questions about these. Provide follow up questions which ask learners to reflect more deeply about what they have learned.
Teacher 6: How can I help children see what they have learned in a lesson?	F Encourage children to share and help each other in pairs and groups. Ask stronger learners to help weaker learners when appropriate.

Match the teachers' questions **1–6** with the possible responses **A–F**.

Reflect: What alternative answers could you give to these teachers? Choose two or three and note your ideas, based on your reading in this unit.

REFLECTION

 Arrange to meet other teachers in your institution, school or context, if possible. Alternatively, you could meet online or do this task in an online group or forum with teachers in another context. Do the task together.

1 What learning strategies have you successfully used yourself to learn English or another language?
2 How do you help children develop learning strategies in your lessons?
3 Put all your ideas from Question 2 together. Which strategies are or might be most useful to young learners of English in your context? Rank the top five or six ideas.
4 Read the following comments about learning strategies. Discuss how far you agree or disagree with them when keeping your own learners in mind:

> *'Children without learning strategies are learners without tools for successful learning.'*
>
> *'The number of learning strategies children have is not important. What is important is how they use and combine the learning strategies they do have.'*

DISCOVERY ACTIVITY

 Look at the following discovery activities to explore the use of learning strategies in your context. Choose two or three which are most useful to you. If you are not a practising young learner teacher right now, you could work with another teacher and their class.

1 Plan for a KWL strategy in your next lesson or unit. Keep a note of the KWL charts developed by the children. Then try the KWL strategy again, at least one more time, and compare the results. Think about how the children have developed learning strategies, and where they may need extra help. Continue with the strategy for a term or longer period, giving the help needed. At the end of that time, do you notice any change in their learning strategies?
2 Plan for a Plan – Do – Review model in your next lesson. Keep notes on learners' responses at each of the stages alongside your *lesson plan*. Afterwards, review those notes to see if you could improve the way you implemented it. Then plan to use it again; repeat as necessary so that you develop a way to use the model to its best effect with your learners.
3 Think about the learners in one of your classes. Which learning strategies can and do most of them use, and which ones do they need help in developing? How can you provide this help?
4 Look at a lesson or activity you will teach soon in your coursebook. Identify two or more learning strategies that children will need to use in order to learn more successfully in the lesson/activity. Plan and teach your lesson and reflect on what you learned about children's use of learning strategies. How can you help your learners improve or develop learning strategies that would help them in this kind of activity?

5 Ask children to brainstorm in groups the strategies they use outside of the classroom to learn or simply encounter English. They could share their ideas with the class by making a poster for display. As you give feedback to the class, provide any extra suitable strategies they haven't thought of.

You can use your TKT: YL PD Journal to record and keep track of this investigation. Remember to follow any ethical procedures required by your institution and to ensure you have informed consent of your learners and other participants before collecting any classroom data.

■ TKT: YL Practice task

 Do the practice task for this unit. Time yourself to see how long you take to answer all the questions.
Then check your answers in the answer key on page 158.

For questions **1–6**, look at the learning strategies and the three classroom activities listed **A–C**.

Choose the classroom activity (**A–C**) which matches the learning strategy.

---

1 Planning learning

  A The teacher asks children what they know about giraffes and what they want to find out.

  B The teacher asks children whether they like giraffes and have seen one at a zoo.

  C The teacher asks children what a giraffe looks like and where it lives.

2 Developing hypotheses about language rules

  A The teacher asks children to guess the title of a story from a picture she shows them.

  B The teacher asks children to say how they think a story about a gardener and a princess will end.

  C The teacher asks children to underline past tense verbs in a story and tell her how they are formed.

3 Setting learning objectives

  A At the start of the lesson about colours, children tell each other all the colour words in English that they know.

  B At the start of the lesson about colours, children say how many colour words they think they can learn in the lesson.

  C At the start of the lesson about colours, children test each other on the spellings of five colour words.

4 Selecting activities

  A In a lesson about sports, children choose which partner they would like to work with.

  B In a lesson about sports, children choose whether to answer a quiz or play a guessing game.

  C In a lesson about sports, children choose which is their favourite sport.

5 Reviewing

   A   At the end of the lesson, the teacher gives children time to think about what they have learned.

   B   At the end of the lesson, the teacher gives children time to talk about their weekend.

   C   At the end of the lesson, the teacher gives children time to copy the homework task from the board.

6 Using reference resources

   A   Children take it in turns to write true sentences about their families on the board.

   B   Children make a family tree and form groups to talk about the people in their family.

   C   Children use picture dictionaries to check that they know the words for different family members.

Unit 3 Developing thinking skills: How can I help children develop cognitive strategies in language learning?

LEARNING OUTCOMES

By the end of this unit, you will...
KNOWLEDGE: know more about the role of language learning in helping children to develop cognitive strategies
SKILLS: be able to identify a range of cognitive strategies and ways of helping children to develop them through language learning

Starter Question

Before you begin this unit, read the starter question and make some notes. Then read the commentary and compare it to your notes.

 What does the term 'cognitive strategy' mean to you? **Use a dictionary to check if you need to.**

COMMENTARY

Cognition is a word meaning *thinking,* so cognitive strategies are the mental skills children use in order to process and understand the content or the language they are learning. As children practise using cognitive skills in different ways, they will be able to develop them for use outside of language learning. For example, they might **predict** what happens next part of the way through a story, or **deduce the meaning** of an unknown word they hear from the **context** in which they meet it.

Cognitive strategies are important because they are essential to children's learning in all school **subjects**. Helping children to develop cognitive strategies while they are learning English therefore plays an important part in children's general development as learners and thinkers. Thinking skills development is seen as one of the '4Cs', which are the four main life skills children need to develop to help them be prepared for their future as adults in the 21st century: Communication, Collaboration, Critical Thinking and Creativity.

Key concepts

Reflect on the *key concept* question. Brainstorm your ideas, then expand your notes as you read.

 What are the cognitive skills and what kinds of strategies might children use to practise them? **Try to think of three or four examples.**

Part of Bloom's Taxonomy, first published in the 1950s, identified cognitive domains and put six related *goals* in order of complexity. This was later revised and is now often presented in a hierarchical triangle (see Figure 1) to show how the goals build upon one another. For example, as part of the cognitive process of evaluating something, we need first to understand and analyse it.

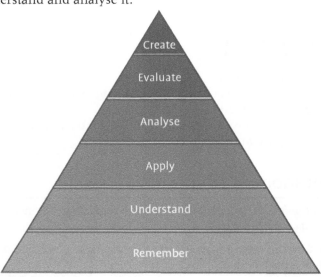

Figure 1: Bloom's Revised Taxonomy of cognitive goals (Anderson & Bloom, 2001).

The three lower levels of the triangle are also sometimes referred to as *Lower Order Thinking Skills* (LOTS), which involve basic gathering and memorisation of information, while the upper three require **Higher Order Thinking Skills** (HOTS), which involve deeper and fuller understanding, processing and application of knowledge.

Children need opportunities to practise and use cognitive strategies when they learn English so that they can develop their abilities as thinkers. Their thinking skills develop as they mature, so younger children are less adept at HOTS than older children, but we can help children develop cognitive strategies involving both LOTS and HOTS even at the younger age range. Classroom activities and teacher language **graded** to the children's age and **developmental** level can help all 6- to 12-year-old children practise and develop cognitive skills. Look at the examples in the table below, which are ranked broadly from least to most complex.

Cognitive strategies	Bloom's Taxonomy level	Classroom activities which help children develop cognitive strategies include:	Example teacher language
identifying	Level 1: Remembering	• labelling visuals • naming objects in the classroom • finding vocabulary items in a short supplementary or coursebook text	*Look at the jungle picture and find three animals. Which animals can you see?*

skimming	Up to level 2: Understanding	• reading quickly or listening once to get the general meaning of a text (e.g. story, song, **chant**)	*Read the dialogue very quickly and tell me if Yuki is happy or sad.*
scanning	Up to level 2: Understanding	• reading or listening to find and understand specific information in a text	*Read the game instructions and tell me how many people can play.*
categorising	Up to level 2: Understanding	• putting things with the same characteristics into groups	*Look at these animals. Are they pets or wild animals? Speak to your partner and make a pets list and a wild animals list.*

matching	Up to level 3: Applying	• putting together:
		  – words and pictures
		  – questions and answers
		  – half-sentences to make complete sentences
			If you have an animal picture card, find your partner, who has the word card for the same animal.

sequencing	Up to level 4: Analysing	• putting events or steps in the order in which they happened	*Listen to the recipe again and put these steps in the right order.*
predicting	Up to level 4: Analysing	• using context to guess what will happen next in a story • using a picture or key words to guess what a song will be about • using context to guess the next line in a **dialogue**	*Look at this forest. Who will the boys find in the forest? What do you think?*
ranking	Up to level 5: Evaluating	• putting things in a set order (this order could be based on fact, opinion, preference, etc.)	*Look at this list of five types of transport. Number them in order from fastest (number 1) to slowest (number 5).*
deducing meaning from context	Up to level 5: Evaluating	• guessing the meaning of unknown words	*Look at the picture and the other words in the sentence: is 'dangerous' something good or bad?*
risk-taking	Up to level 6: Creating	• using **hypotheses** about language to say or write something the child hasn't been formally taught yet in English	*OK, you know the words dancer and teacher... So, what do we call a person who writes books?*
creating	Up to level 6: Creating	• making something new based on understanding or knowledge • using different materials and resources to make something new	*Make a list of important words in our environment topic. Use the words to create a word puzzle, like a crossword or wordsearch with clues.*

■ Key concepts and the YL classroom

> Reflect on the *key concepts and the YL classroom* question. Brainstorm your ideas, then expand your notes as you read.
>
> *How can teachers use questions to help learners develop thinking skills?* **Note two or three ideas.**

COMMENTARY

There are many ways teachers use questions in their classrooms, such as to check understanding, to see how well children are meeting learning *objectives* or to check children's reaction or feelings. We can see that asking questions is a key teacher skill.

Different question types can serve different purposes. For example, simple yes/no questions, or questions which ask children to give short factual answers (*closed questions*) have a useful role in the young learner classroom because they allow children to develop confidence in their ability to understand and to produce language. They also help the teacher to check children's comprehension. Children have big imaginations and plenty of ideas, and so need opportunities to put their own thoughts into words. That is why it is also very important for teachers to ask *open questions* when appropriate. Open questions do not have a right or wrong answer, so they provide children with an opportunity to develop their thinking by expressing their own ideas. If children are listening to a story about a boy who is lost, for example, the teacher might stop the recording, and ask: *How can he find his way home?* If they are going to read a simple *graded reader* about elephants, the teacher might ask: *What would you like to find out about elephants?* Open questions often allow children to process language at a deeper emotional level than simple yes/no questions, and so make language memorable and learning interesting. They can also stimulate children's thinking at a deeper level, for example when asked to give and justify an opinion.

Teachers can also help children to develop cognitive strategies by allowing *wait time* after they ask open questions. Children need time to check that they have understood a question, that they can answer it, and to think about the words they need to explain their thinking. Fisher (2005, p. 23) explains that allowing children three seconds or longer to think before answering a question can result in more children in a class who are willing to answer, and responses which are longer, more thoughtful and imaginative than when an immediate answer is required. Strategies such as **Think-Pair-Share,** where children first think for themselves, then check their ideas with a partner before sharing it with a bigger group or the whole class, are also effective in giving thinking time (wait time).

It is quite common that one or two learners dominate classroom interaction, perhaps by often shouting out answers, always having their hand held high (and eager). It is important, therefore, to *nominate* different learners, giving them the opportunity to be heard, to contribute actively and help you gauge their progress and understanding of language. This will prevent the dominant students from answering everything, and can encourage all the students to think if you ask the question first, give a little wait time, then nominate someone to answer it. This will also give you the opportunity to *differentiate*, as you can nominate different learners for different kinds of question, give more or less wait time and so on, depending on the ability of the learner you nominate.

Exploring the concepts in practice

 FOLLOW-UP ACTIVITY *(see page 149 for answers)*

> **Look at the two coursebook extracts and identify the cognitive strategies they involve for learners.**

Extract 1:

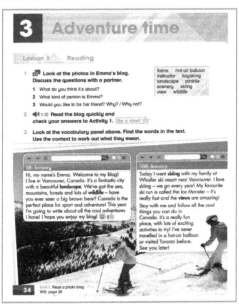

Which cognitive strategies do the activities in Extract 1 require learners to use? Choose more than one answer:

A Sequencing
B Skimming
C Creating
D Predicting
E Deducing meaning from context

Extract from Elsworth and Rose (2017) *Academy Stars* Pupil's Book 5, p. 34: Macmillan Education

Extract 2:

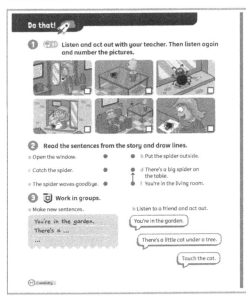

Which cognitive strategies do the activities in Extract 2 require learners to use? Choose more than one answer:

A Sequencing
B Creating
C Predicting
D Ranking
E Risk-taking
F Scanning

Extract from Williams, Putcha, Gerngross and Lewis-Jones (2022) *Super Minds* Student's Book 1, p. 92: Cambridge University Press & Assessment

REFLECTION

Read these teachers' comments. How would you respond to each teacher?

> **Teacher 1:** I try to include both simple factual questions and open questions in my lessons when I can.

> **Teacher 2:** Open questions are a good idea, but children don't have enough English to answer them.

> **Teacher 3:** A good answer is worth waiting for.

> **Teacher 4:** I like the idea of wait time, but I think silence will feel uncomfortable. I think it's better to fill silences with praise or a comment, or just move to the next learner.

DISCOVERY ACTIVITY

Follow the steps to investigate about questions and wait time in your classroom practice.

Find out about your practice: Questions and wait time

Step 1: Choose an activity or topic you are going to use soon in class. Plan some appropriate closed questions and open questions to ask which will encourage children to use HOTS as well as LOTS.

Step 2: Teach the class. Remember to use wait time after you ask your questions. Focus on children's responses to your questions. Make brief notes about children's responses to your questions (mental or on paper) during the class and spend a short time immediately afterwards to expand your records and notes.

Step 3: As soon as possible after the lesson, spend time looking through your notes. Think about:
1 whether children's answers to the open questions showed evidence of their thinking.
2 whether wait time produced more participation from children.
3 whether there were differences in children's responses to closed or open questions.
4 what difficulties occurred and how you dealt with them.
5 what you have learned from using open questions and wait time.

Step 4: Set yourself one or two action points to improve your questioning in your classroom practice, for example:
- To give one or two seconds more wait time when I ask open questions.
- To give children the opportunity to share or discuss their answer with a partner before nominating a student to share their answer with the class.

You can use your TKT: YL PD Journal to record and keep track of this investigation. Remember to follow any ethical procedures required by your institution and to ensure you have informed consent of your learners and other participants before collecting any classroom data.

■ TKT: YL Practice task

 Do the practice task for this unit. Time yourself to see how long you take to answer all the questions.
Then check your answers in the answer key on page 158.

For questions **1–6**, match the teachers' descriptions of classroom tasks involving pictures with the main cognitive strategies they focus on listed **A–C**.

Choose the correct letter (**A–C**).

Main cognitive strategies

A categorising
B sequencing
C predicting

Classroom tasks involving pictures

1 I asked children to look at the picture and tell me which activities are healthy and which activities are bad for your health.

2 I showed children one half of a picture of a house and asked them to guess what was in the other half.

3 As children listened to a song about a friendly dinosaur, they put three pictures describing the story in the right order.

4 Children looked at a picture of a forest, two children and a river, and told me what they thought the story would be about.

5 Children read a recipe for mushroom omelette and numbered pictures to describe the correct steps for making the omelette.

6 Children helped me to put the sports flashcards into two piles: summer and winter sports.

Unit 4   Developing communication skills: How can I help children develop communication strategies through language learning?

LEARNING OUTCOMES

By the end of this unit, you will...
KNOWLEDGE: know more about language and non-language strategies commonly used in communication
SKILLS: be able to identify a range of communication strategies and ways of helping children to develop them through language learning

■ Starter Question

Before you begin this unit, read the starter question and make some notes. Then read the commentary and compare it to your notes.

 ***What do people use in order to communicate?* List as many points as you can.**

COMMENTARY

When people interact with one another, they communicate using words and other non-language tools. We begin communicating the moment we are born – babies communicate their basic human needs to their parent or carer: *I'm hungry! Something hurts! I want a hug!* They do this by crying and cooing. As we grow up, we begin to convey information more precisely – older babies will begin to use simple words, like *More!*, gestures such as reaching, and later, pointing. These usually become more intentional strategies before a child's first birthday. Later, our communication becomes more sophisticated, and we can express our needs more precisely and clearly. We become more skilled at communicating using both words and non-language tools, such as gestures, voice, **facial expression**. For example, to communicate a need for help, we may use the word *Help!,* but are likely to shout it in a tone of voice which reflects the degree of urgency. We might wave an arm and wear an expression of fear or shock, all depending on the situation.

A **function** is the reason or purpose for using language, e.g. *making a suggestion; giving advice* (*TKT Glossary*, p. 18) and, therefore, functional language is the particular words, **chunks** or phrases that we use to perform different actions. This language can be categorised in different ways, for example:

1 *Personal expression* (e.g. talking about yourself, introducing yourself, expressing feelings and emotions)
2 *Social interaction* (e.g. greeting and introducing people, thanking people, saying goodbye)
3 *Conversation skills* (e.g. asking for clarification, asking someone to speak more slowly or to explain more clearly)
4 *Explaining, giving and asking for information* (e.g. getting information, describing something, answering requests for information)
5 *Expressing an opinion* (e.g. talking about likes, dislikes and preferences, agreeing and disagreeing, accepting or refusing)
6 *Getting something done* (e.g. asking about something, asking for permission, buying something)

These functions can take place in various situations and in interactions with different people. Younger children may be less experienced in these kinds of interaction than older children or adults, and may have more limited language resources at their disposal. As with the other kinds of strategy we talked about in Units 2 and 3, helping children develop interaction skills is important for their overall development, regardless of the language they use. We can support children of all ages in becoming more skilled in communicating in English by helping them develop communication strategies, which they can use to support their communication. These are intentional or unplanned actions used by a speaker to support them in the communication of meaning. They may be verbal (e.g. use of chunks or functional language), phonological (e.g. tone of voice, word or sentence stress) or non-verbal (e.g. gestures, facial expression).

◼ Key concepts

> Reflect on the *key concept* question. Brainstorm your ideas, then expand your notes as you read.
>
> *What kinds of strategy for communication do/would you teach your young learners?* **Think of as many as you can.**

COMMENTARY

When our students practise using language in a ***communicative activity***, they need to use some form of communication strategy in the same way that people almost always use communication strategies in everyday life. Speakers often use these strategies without thinking or unintentionally, but young language learners may need to notice and try to use these more deliberately, at least until they become more automatic for them. Added to this, some non-verbal strategies may be unique to or differ in meaning or nuance between specific cultures, such as the hand gesture to beckon in Japanese or the South Asian head shake.

There are four types of strategy, and each has different features or involves particular considerations:

Verbal (spoken)

- Choice of words, e.g. use of adult/typical children's words, *colloquial* language or slang
- Level of *formality*
- Pitch and tone of voice
- Speed of delivery
- Clarity of meaning

Verbal (written)

- Choice of words, e.g. use of adult's/typical children's words, use of colloquial language or slang
- Level of formality (as appropriate to genre)
- Use of *fixed expressions* or conventions for specific genres (e.g. email openings, use of internet language, e.g. LOL, BFF)
- Structure (at word, sentence and paragraph level)
- Clarity of meaning

Communication strategies

Non-verbal

- Facial expressions
- Posture
- Gestures and touching
- Eye contact
- Culturally-specific features (e.g. particular gestures or body language used in a culture)

Visual

- Visuals such as emoticons, GIFs, images, video clips, drawings etc. to support or replace verbal strategies,
- Appropriacy of content (e.g. age, culture)

When we are using a second or foreign language, we may need to rely on more non-verbal or different verbal strategies to interact with other people than we are used to using in our everyday interactions. At a beginning stage, these may be survival strategies, but will continue to be strategies such as using a gesture to support meaning or asking someone to repeat if you don't understand something or your conversation partner is speaking too fast for you. Learners can develop these through communicative language practice activities, but we can also explicitly teach important communication strategies.

In a language learning classroom, it is assumed that the learners and perhaps the teacher are speakers of another language. In a monolingual classroom, that is one where learners all speak the same first language, this language then becomes a tool for communicating in English. In the language classroom, mediation is a communication strategy where learners or the teacher use the other language to support their communication. This may involve, for example, using or translating some words or explaining a concept in the L1 to another learner who needs help understanding something. A language learner's first language will not go away, so it is important to show learners how to use it as a communication strategy. This will help them become more confident in communicating in real-life situations in the future.

Key concepts and the YL classroom

Reflect on the *key concepts and the YL classroom* question. Brainstorm your ideas, then expand your notes as you read.

 What kinds of classroom activity are suitable for teaching communication strategies to young learners? **Think of two or three examples.**

COMMENTARY

Here are some examples of ways in which we can explicitly teach communication strategies:

Classroom language posters
Learners work in groups to **brainstorm** useful classroom language in English; this is likely to be functional language. The teacher's role is to suggest ideas as necessary and to help the children express the words and phrases accurately.
Children gather their classroom language examples together and write them on a poster. This could be a group or **whole-class** poster. They could illustrate the poster to show meaning or they could add a translation.
Learners practise the language first by repeating it, with attention paid to appropriate pitch, tone and relevant non-verbal strategies, before doing a **practice activity**. Later, children can refer to the poster when they want to communicate something in the classroom.

Example classroom language poster (Shin, et al. (2021) p. 43)

Learners could also write their own checklist of phrases and expressions. Each time they use one of these, they can tick it on their checklist. At the end of each class, week or unit, they can share the phrases they have used (and not used).

The example classroom language poster shown may have been written by the teacher or collaboratively produced by a group or whole class of students. With younger learners who are not able to read, the poster could show gestures or mimes which prompt children to combine with learned phrases and expressions.

Role plays with a communication checklist

Before children do a **role play** activity, the teacher can brainstorm useful or important functional expressions or chunks of language as a whole class. For example, the children are going to do a role play where they buy an ice-cream in a shop. The teacher may **elicit** ways to greet the shop assistant, to ask politely for something or to say thank you and goodbye. They can be practised as part of a **model** dialogue before learners devise their own role play exchange. When **pairs** perform their role plays in groups or to the class, the rest of the class can use a checklist of phrases (e.g. the language brainstormed earlier in the lesson) to see which ones the pairs use in their dialogue. They can use this to give **peer feedback**.

Communication without words

There are numerous games young learners can play in the classroom where they need to communicate without using words. These include miming games (gestures), drawing games (visual), or emoticon games (facial expression) and can involve children trying to communicate a word or message through non-verbal means, while others guess what is being communicated and/or respond in an appropriate way (verbally or even non-verbally). For example, children work in pairs. One child looks at a card which reads 'Say hello!'. The child should gesture the message to communicate with their partner, e.g. by waving, shaking hands or bowing. The partner should respond verbally, e.g. by saying 'Hi! How are you?' or 'Nice to meet you!'. Alternatively, learners look at a set of emoticons, choose one and do the facial expression to show the emotion shown. The other children guess which emoticon their classmate is performing.

Drama activities

Using **drama** in the classroom brings many benefits, including helping children think creatively, to build self-confidence and self-esteem and to find and use their own voice (See Hillyard, 2016, for more about using drama to support English language learning). It can also support children as they practise all kinds of communication strategies, both those using words and those without words. In drama, we may exaggerate non-verbal strategies, for example, while verbal strategies can be incorporated into the script. The script, in turn, can be adjusted to support this by the teacher or written by the children themselves.

Collaborative groupwork

When working in **collaborative** groups, children will need to utilise a number of communication strategies in order to collaborate as a group member and move the group task forward. This may especially be the case when children work on **projects** or **problem-solving tasks**. They may need to express their ideas clearly, ask for clarification, agree, disagree, protest, suggest and so on. Some children, especially younger children or children who lack confidence, may need extra support with communication strategies for group work. Functional language or non-verbal strategies could be introduced, practised, then put on a checklist before collaborative group activities begin. This may involve images, such as emoticons, question marks, a hand up, which may indicate agree, disagree, question, suggest and so on, or it may be a list of chunks or expressions. A rule allowing only two or three of each to be ticked off during an activity will help manage dominant learners and support shy children.

■ Exploring the concepts in practice

FOLLOW-UP ACTIVITY *(see page 150 for answers)*

 Read about three well-known, commonly played games which can be used to teach English to young learners. Answer the question.

Game 1: *Happy families*

We usually play this card game in groups of four. The pack of 16 cards includes cards showing various members of different families. Players start with four cards and try to collect all four from the same family by, in turns, picking a card from the pile or asking another player for one of their cards, e.g. *'Do you have someone from the Smith family?'* The player asked should give their card if they have one and say, for example, *'Yes, here you are'*. Other language in the game might include: *'I'm sorry, I can't help you'*, *'It's your/my turn'* or *'Could you repeat that, please?'*

In the young learner English classroom, the families might be replaced by words from different **lexical sets** (e.g. animals, transport etc.); older children could use more complex questions, such as *'Do you have a person who works on a farm?'* or be required to respond in more detail.

Game 2: *Charades*

In turns, players think of a book, film or TV show. They first indicate to the other players what type of media it is and how many words make up the title, then they mime the title, either word by word or as a whole. They must not make any sound, give clues, write or mouth words while they mime. The other players should guess the title, by saying, for example, *'Is it...?'* or *'It could be... Am I right?'*. Whoever guesses the title has the next turn to mime.

The game can be played in this way, using familiar books, films and so on. The teacher may decide to provide prompts or ideas for the children to mime. Alternatively, the game could be modified so learners mime characters (e.g. from a story they have been reading as a class), people in different professions and so on.

Game 3: *Hopscotch*

Young children often play this game in the school **playground**, although it can be played in an indoor space too. All you need is a piece of chalk and a stone. Together you draw a hopscotch grid (you can find examples of this online) on the ground, and number the squares one to ten. The learners take turns to throw the stone onto the squares, starting at number one and moving up one each time, and should jump onto all the squares, missing out the one with the stone. If they jump or throw the stone outside the box, they miss a turn. The winner is the first to complete square 10.

They may use particular phrases to manage the team game in English, such as *'Miss a go!'* Or *'It's my go'*. They could also say the numbers or other words or phrases as they jump on the hopscotch squares each time.

Look at communication strategies in the table. Which ones are or could be practised in each of the games? Put ticks in the table. There are several possible strategies for each game.

Communication strategy	Example	Game 1: *Happy families*	Game 2: *Charades*	Game 3: *Hopscotch*
Using functional language to congratulate a winner	*Well done!*			
Using functional language for turn-taking	*It's your turn!*			
Using functional language to give opinion	*I think it's...*			
Using functional language to ask for an object	*Can I have..., please?*			
Using functional language when giving something	*Here you are!*			
Using functional language for collaboration	*Let's...*			
Using visuals	Using numbers; pictures			
Using gestures and body language to explain	Miming			

Answer the reflection questions A and B.

A. Look at these example communication strategies. How might they be useful to children learning English?

1 *Clarifying*
2 *Attracting someone's attention*
3 *Giving a reason*

4 *Asking for information*
5 *Describing an action, routine or appearance*
6 *Asking for permission*

B. Choose three or four of the communication strategies from question A.

a. What language chunks, phrases or expressions in English do/could children need for them?
b. Think of one or two communicative activities which will give children the opportunity to practise each strategy.

DISCOVERY ACTIVITY

 Look at the discovery activities to explore teaching and learning in your context. Do one or two activities which are most useful to you in your context.

1 Look online, in supplementary resource books or packs at games for young English learners. Find a game or activity that you haven't used before, that would be suitable for your learners and that you would like to try in your classroom. Analyse the game/activity – what kinds of communication strategies will the children need to use to play the game/do the activity? How could you introduce these strategies before children play the game, so they can practise them in that game?

2 Arrange a time to meet and talk to other teachers in your school, area or Professional Learning Network. Together, brainstorm the communication strategies that your learners use or could use in their English lessons to help them interact more in English in the classroom.
Share and discuss strategies that have been successful in helping learners with communication strategies.

3 Informally, ***observe*** one or two of your learners in one or more of your lessons. Make a note in your TKT: YL PD Journal of all the communication strategies they used, either in English, their L1, another language or non-verbally.
After the lesson, decide which of these would be useful to teach to the other learners in your class(es) or context.

You can use your TKT: YL PD Journal to record and keep track of this investigation. Remember to follow any ethical procedures required by your institution and to ensure you have informed consent of your learners and other participants before collecting any classroom data.

■ TKT: YL Practice task

 Do the practice task for this unit. Time yourself to see how long you take to answer all the questions.

Then check your answers in the answer key on page 158.

For questions **1–6**, look at the strategies. Two of the example strategies are communication strategies. One strategy is **<u>NOT</u>** a communication strategy.

Decide which strategy (**A–C**) is **not** a communication strategy.

---

1 Which of these strategies is NOT a communication strategy?

   A   Problem solving
   B   Giving your opinion
   C   Using gestures

2 Which of these strategies is NOT a communication strategy?

   A   Disagreeing
   B   Setting learning goals
   C   Adding a smiley to a message

3 Which of these strategies is NOT a communication strategy?

   A   Matching
   B   Describing a personal experience
   C   Describing what someone looks like

4 Which of these strategies is NOT a communication strategy?

   A   Clarifying
   B   Using colloquial language
   C   Skimming

5 Which of these strategies is NOT a communication strategy?

   A   Ranking
   B   Greeting
   C   Nodding

6 Which of these strategies is NOT a communication strategy?

   A   Disagreeing
   B   Smiling
   C   Deducing meaning

Reflection on learning in Part 1

You have come to the end of Part 1. This part of *The TKT Course: Young Learner Module* aimed to deepen your understanding of the characteristics of children aged 6–12 as learners, and guide you in considering the implications of this for teaching English to these learners. This part of *The TKT Course: Young Learner Module* also aimed to support your knowledge and skills in preparation for the first part of the *TKT: YL Module test: Knowledge of young learners and principles of teaching English to young learners*.

Look back to the introduction in Part 1. You assessed your level of understanding before beginning the first unit. Re-assess your understanding in each area.

You also wrote two or three questions or identified areas to find out about in each unit. How well do you think you have achieved these? What can you do to better achieve those areas you need to work on? For example:
- Reread a section of the unit(s).
- Re-do or do more exploration activities (Second C of each unit).
- Discuss the unit(s) content with other teachers in your school or network.
- Re-do the TKT: YL practice task(s).
- Look in the *TKT glossary* or the glossary in this book to check meanings of key terms and concepts you are unsure about.
- Reflect on your classroom teaching more closely.
- Look for other readings or resources on the topic(s).

Write yourself two or three objectives for further learning and development in your TKT: YL PD Journal.

■ References and further recommended reading

PART 1 REFERENCES

Cameron, L. (2001). *Teaching Languages to Young Learners.* Cambridge: Cambridge University Press & Assessment.

Dweck, C.S. (2006). *Mindset. Changing the Way You Think to Fulfil Your Potential.* London: Robinson.

Ellis, G. and Ibrahim, N. (2015). *Teaching Children How to Learn.* Peaslake: DELTA Publishing.

Elsworth, S. and Rose, J. (2017) *Academy Stars*, Pupil's Book 5, p. 34 Oxford: Macmillan Education.

Fisher, R. (2005). *Teaching Children to Learn.* (2nd ed.) Cheltenham: Nelson Thornes.

Halliwell, S. (1992). *Teaching English in the Primary Classroom.* Harlow: Longman.

Hillyard, S. (2016). *English Through Drama: Creative Activities for Inclusive ELT classes*. Innsbruck: Helbling Languages.

Read, C. (2003). Is Younger Better? *English Teaching Professional*. (Issue 28, July 2003). Pp. 5–7.

Shin, J. K., Savić, V. and Machida, T. (2021). *The 6 Principles for Exemplary Teaching of English Learners*. Alexandria: TESOL International Association.

Williams, M. with Puchta, H., Gerngross, G. & Lewis-Jones, P. (2022). *Super Minds*. Student's Book 1. Cambridge: Cambridge University Press & Assessment.

Zapiain, G. (2019) *Cambridge Primary Path*. Student's Book 2. Cambridge: Cambridge University Press & Assessment.

RECOMMENDED FURTHER READING

Pfenniger, S. E. and Singleton, D. (2019). The Age Debate. A Critical Overview. In S. Garton & F. Copland. *The Routledge Handbook of Teaching English to Young learners*. Pp. 30–43. London: Routledge.

Pinter, A (2006). *Teaching Young Language Learners*. Oxford: Oxford University Press.

Puchta, H. and Williams, M. (2018). *Teaching Young Learners to Think. ELT Activities for Young Learners Aged 6–12*. Innsbruck: Helbling Languages.

Rixon, S. (2013). *British Council Survey of Policy and Practice in Primary English Language Teaching World-wide*. London: British Council.

Willis, N. (2018). *Growth Mindset: A Practical Guide*. Sydney: Bloomsbury.

Part 2 | Planning and preparing young learner lessons

Introduction to Part 2

Part 2 aims to enrich awareness and skills in planning and preparing lessons for young learners, including analysing, selecting, adapting and supplementing materials and resources for learning.

This part of *The TKT Course: Young Learner Module* will support your knowledge and skills in preparation for the second part of the *TKT: YL Module test: Planning and preparing young learner lessons*. You can find more information in the *TKT: YL syllabus* in the module handbook, which is available online.

In the first unit of this part, Unit 5, we'll look at lesson planning, thinking about what to take into consideration when planning for young learner lessons. You'll think about what a **lesson plan** is, how it might look, and why planning is important, particularly for young learner lessons. Then, you'll look at what a lesson plan might contain.

Unit 6 turns to classroom materials. You will find out about different types of teaching and learning materials and think about deciding factors when choosing materials. Finally in this unit, you'll reflect on some issues we may have with materials and how we might change the material to address these issues.

In the next unit, Unit 7, you will find out more about selecting, adapting and supplementing classroom **learning resources**. This unit will ask you to think about why we use additional resources in young learner classrooms, how we can use them to enrich learning and better meet the needs of our learners. The final section of this unit considers how some additional resources may differ or be used differently with younger and older children in the 6–12 age group.

Towards the end of each unit, you will find follow-up activities, which are designed to deepen and extend your thinking in relation to the unit content. These will help you reflect on the classroom application of your learning in your own context. These are followed by a set of TKT: YL practice questions based on the unit theme. It is recommended that you use your TKT: YL PD Journal to keep and organise your notes.

As you did in Part 1, look at the **can-do statements** before you begin the units in Part 2. Evaluate your own understanding and skills for each one. After completing Part 2, return to these and re-assess yourself. From that, you can develop an action plan to continue focusing on any particular areas you feel necessary.

SELF-ASSESSMENT

Unit	Rate yourself from: 1 (*Limited or not at all*) **to 5** (*This is a strength*)	Rating before Part 2	Rating after Part 2
5	*I can* identify key features of a lesson plan and say why they are important factors to consider in planning.		
6	*I can* analyse materials and find solutions for potential problems in use with a group of children.		
7	*I can* identify and select appropriate resources for a specific teaching context or moment.		

In your TKT: YL PD Journal, identify two or three questions or areas you'd like to know more about in each unit in Part 2. When you have finished Part 2, return to these to see if you have answered them. If you haven't, read around the topic using the recommended reading list at the end of Part 1. You can also find many resources for teacher professional development online.

Unit 5 Lesson planning: What do I need to think about when planning language lessons for children?

LEARNING OUTCOMES

By the end of this unit, you will...
KNOWLEDGE: know how and why teachers prepare lessons using lesson plan documentation
SKILLS: be able to identify key features of an effective young learner lesson plan

■ Starter Question

Before you begin this unit, read the starter questions and make some notes. Then read the commentary and compare it to your notes.

 What is a lesson plan? Do all teachers' lesson plans look the same?

COMMENTARY

A lesson plan is a document which outlines the learning that the teacher hopes or expects will take place in a lesson. For the teacher, it serves as a guide, map or instructions for a lesson, which has been prepared with a number of key considerations in mind so that learners are most likely to meet the ***lesson aims*** and ***objectives.***

Teachers hold different views on lesson planning, and their lesson plans may look different on paper (or computer), depending on their background: their training as well as the length and type of their teaching experience and teaching context. However, before beginning a class, an effective teacher will have a clear idea of what they are going to teach, what their learners will gain from the lesson (content and skills) and how they are going to teach the lesson in order for that to happen. Some teachers' lesson plans are less detailed and include less varied information than others', although effective teachers consider similar questions when deciding what and how to teach their class.

We will see in this unit that lesson planning has an impact on the success of children's learning as well as on teachers' own development. Lesson plans are not only a plan for upcoming lessons, but can also be used for reflection on a lesson or series of lessons. In cases where a teacher teaches the same lesson multiple times to different groups, or the same course year after year or term after term, the lesson plans can be revised and reused for successive courses.

■ Key concepts

> Reflect on the *key concept* question. Brainstorm your ideas, then expand your notes as you read.
>
> *What are your reasons for planning your lessons?* **List at least four reasons.**

COMMENTARY

It is important for all teachers to plan their lessons, and there are many reasons for this which relate to the teacher and teaching or the learner and learning. Moon (2000, pp. 100–101) usefully categorises these into four broad areas:

Practical reasons

Practical reasons refer to the importance of the plan as a guide or support in helping the teacher before and during the lesson. This includes planning what to prepare and take to the lesson (*handouts*, additional resources, etc.), computer hardware or software to set-up, as well as what to do at each step (*stage*) of the lesson (outlined in the lesson *procedure* part of the plan), how long it should take and how to manage or *differentiate* learning for children during the lesson. In other words, the plan serves as a reminder in the classroom so that the different stages of the lesson happen at the right time, in the right order and in an organised, well-managed and coherent way, which creates conditions for children to learn effectively and efficiently. Systematic planning will help ensure that a *syllabus* and/or *curriculum* objectives can be met. A teacher who has planned thoroughly is, therefore, likely to have confidence in themselves and their teaching; in turn, the learners can trust in that teacher and know that their language lessons will help them learn what they expect to learn. This inspires positive behaviour and *motivation* in learners.

Finally, a well-written, detailed lesson plan can also be re-used or used by another teacher, which can be valuable when teachers repeat lessons, work in groups, share lesson plans or perhaps need to cover for a colleague who is sick or unable to teach a class.

Professional development

As mentioned in the previous section, lesson plans can serve as a document or data for teacher reflection and self-evaluation after teaching a lesson. The teacher can do this by *monitoring* and reflecting on their own teaching performance in order to identify ways in which they can improve. The teacher can use it to see whether the lesson objectives have been achieved, for example, and if not, consider why not. Systematic reflection on a lesson plan is essential for identifying where a lesson might need to be adapted for subsequent uses, either in order to make it suitable for different individuals or classes, or to improve it in a more fundamental way.

Accountability

Lesson plans can also serve as evidence of teaching which allows for transparency. Documentation of lesson planning is sometimes required by an institution or school for their records, for quality assurance, for **school inspectors** or for parents/caregivers. In some contexts, for example, teachers plan lessons for a unit, theme or school term in advance and make these plans available to parents/caregivers so that they know and understand more about what happens in their children's English lessons.

Confidence

Lastly, but importantly, planning can make teachers more confident about their teaching. This can come from being better organised and prepared, and also from a feeling of ownership and control over their own professional development and learning as well as over their classroom. When working with children, the level of a teacher's confidence plays a particularly key part in effective *classroom management* and learner *attitude*. As mentioned previously, a teacher who delivers a smooth, well-planned lesson, who has everything ready, is decisive and doesn't hesitate, get lost or become confused, will have greater authority in the classroom and gain more respect from the learners. As a result, the learners will usually be more attentive, focused and respond more positively to the teacher as they trust the teacher to be in control and find themselves in a safe, secure learning environment.

■ Key concepts and the YL classroom

> Reflect on the *key concepts and the YL classroom* question. Brainstorm your ideas, then expand your notes as you read.
>
> **What do you need to ask yourself when planning your YL lessons? List at least three questions.**

COMMENTARY

There are many questions to ask ourselves when planning a lesson. We need to think about what, how, how long and, of course, why to teach – always keeping our learners central in our thinking. Consider the questions to ask yourself in this four-step process:

Step one: Deciding what to teach

Syllabus fit & previous learning	• Where are the learners in their course (early on, near the end, etc.)? • What have learners already/just learned? (language and/or topic) • Do they need to review or redo this learning? • If not, what comes next in the syllabus or **coursebook**? • Do they need everything that comes next in the syllabus or coursebook? • Are they interested in what comes next?*
Lesson objectives & learning **outcomes**	• What do I want this lesson to achieve, specifically (lesson objectives)? • What do I want my learners to get from this lesson, specifically (learning outcomes)?

*Note: Although we may be guided by course material such as a coursebook, it is always important to consider any changes to that material which will help our particular learners learn best. We will focus on this later in Units 6 and 7.

Step two: Deciding how to teach it

At this stage, we can begin to plan the procedure of the lesson, that is we decide on the best activities to use and how to sequence them so that learners build their understanding and skills throughout the lesson, meet the lesson objectives and achieve the learning outcomes. We should consider how to: open the lesson, introduce the topic, find out what learners already know, present language in a relevant *context*, have learners work with the new language, provide different kinds of *practice* activity and *interaction patterns* (pair work, group work, individual work), and so on. Again, we may be guided by a syllabus or coursebook, but we should always consider what is best and most engaging for our learners.

Step three: Fine-tuning the lesson plan
Certain questions will also need reflecting upon when deciding on the details of the lesson procedure, to be sure your lesson plan is effective and practically helpful.

Learning resources	• What equipment will I need to teach the lesson? (e.g. equipment such as an *interactive whiteboard* (IWB), student tablets, internet connection) • What other resources do I need, and how many? (e.g. handouts – one per pair, *flashcard* sets, *realia (real things)*, reference materials, audio/video files, student-made resources)
Interaction patterns	• What kind of interaction will happen at each stage of the lesson (e.g. individual, pair work, group work)? • Is there a good balance of different interaction types?
Differentiation	• How can I support children who may have difficulty with language or ideas? • How can I challenge children whose language level is high? • How can I incorporate different activty types and/or offer choice of activity or product?
Assessment evidence	• How will I know if the learners are meeting / have met the lesson objectives? (e.g. an activity which I can monitor to see how well learners use new language or skills; questions for a quick *scan* to check *achievement*, such as hands-up or traffic-lights [see Part 4 for more on this strategy])

| Problems and solutions | • Problem: What might my learners have difficulty doing or saying? (e.g. spelling a particular word); What could go wrong? (e.g. learners might not understand such complicated game rules; they may not want to work together)
• Solution: How can I plan to avoid or address the problem? (e.g. show the written word on the IWB or on a flashcard so learners can copy it if they need to; simplify the game; have learners choose their own partners) |

Step four: Finishing the planning process
Finally, in order to complete our lesson planning, we will also need to think about:

| Follow-up suggestions | • How might learners review, extend or further practise the **target language** in the next lesson(s)?
• (How) is this lesson preparing learners for the next lesson(s)? (e.g. preparing for a **project**; providing basic topic-related vocabulary or content)
• Do I need to ask learners to prepare for the next lesson? (e.g. to review, do an **at-home task**, bring something from home next time) |

| Personal teaching aim | • What aspect of my classroom teaching can I focus on improving? (e.g. using questions to support learning; projecting my voice) |

| Lesson evaluation | • Leave space on the lesson plan to make notes and comments during the lesson about how well it goes, any unexpected problems or ideas for improvement.
• Include a space at the end to write a short summary to evaluate what went well and what problems arose, after the lesson. |

■ Exploring the concepts in practice

FOLLOW-UP ACTIVITY *(see page 151 for answers)*

 Look at the teacher's plan for a Grade 3 class. Match the elements from the box below to the content of the plan (numbers *1–10). Note there are two extra elements.

Elements:

Personal teaching aim	Differentiation	Learning resources	Follow-up suggestions
Extension activity	Learning outcomes	Lesson evaluation	Possible problems and solutions
Assessment evidence	Procedure	Syllabus fit and previous learning	Interaction patterns

Teacher's lesson plan:

Lesson plan Part A **Class:** *Lion Class* (Grade 3; 15 children, aged around 8 years) **Date:** 28th June	
*1	Unit 5, Lesson 3. Speaking and listening practice of language and vocabulary introduced in Lessons 1 and 2. Learners have already encountered target language and key vocabulary.
*2	By the end of the lesson, learners will have practised describing people's appearance in a group speaking activity using *(S)he has a...* (+ noun); *(S)he is...* (+ adjective).
*3	Sets of 'people' flashcards (1 set per group of four children) Bingo card (1 per child); blank bingo cards (1 per child); Set of people pictures to show on the screen Coloured pens and pencils
*4	Some children may take a long time to draw pictures, while others may find it difficult to choose and write appropriate words. // Set a clear time limit; Give students the choice to draw or write, or a combination of both. If some learners are having difficulty, suggest that they choose one or more flashcards from the people set to put on their bingo card. Two children in the class often only want to work with their friends, but they would benefit from trying to work with other children too. // Use a strategy such as *apples-pears-bananas* to assign groups (e.g. deal out flashcards of particular things/categories or have students take coloured blocks of specific colours from a bag, then all the students with the same flashcard, category or item make a group), reminding children they can return to their seats after the activity. Monitor carefully and offer support where needed.
*5	I want to take care when I set up activities to be sure that I get children's attention before giving instructions, that I check my instructions and that children are able to use the target language so that they can all participate in the activity in English.

Lesson plan Part B			*6: _____
Stage	**Teacher notes and actions**	**Learner action**	***7** _____
Warmer (5–10 mins)	Greetings **routine**	Children sing *Hello, how are you?* song and respond **chorally** and individually.	Ss (whole class) S (individual) T-S (individual)
	Play guessing game *Who is it?* – describe a student in the class	Children guess who the teacher is describing	
Review **target language** (10 mins)	Play bingo. Note how students respond to the target language (***8** _____). Review further if necessary.	Children listen to the description of the people, find the picture on their bingo card and cross it off.	T-S
Speaking activity preparation (10 mins)	Show the set of people pictures on the screen. As a class, elicit then match the key words (adjectives and nouns) to each picture by dragging and dropping. Show children how to choose six people. They can choose to draw, write or use a flashcard, depending on their preference or ability (***9** _____).	Children look, read and match words to pictures on the screen. Children choose six people from the screen. They add the people onto a new bingo card how they like (by drawing or describing using words). They could use one or more of the people flashcards to put on their bingo card if time is short (***9** _____).	Ss S
Speaking activity (10–15 mins)	Demonstrate how to play bingo in groups. Review target language and check instructions. Monitor and listen to students as they use the target language; note how well they work with their classmates in groups (***8** _____).	Children take turns in their group to describe a person. They cross off the person they hear, if they have it on their bingo card. The winner is the first to make a line.	S-Ss (Groups)
Feedback (5–10 mins)	Conduct **whole class** feedback and review common mistakes using a game-like error correction activity.	Children feed back on the activity and participate in error correction game.	Ss-T
Closure (5–10 mins)	Exit tickets – ask children to complete today's exit ticket (***8** _____).	Children write in their notebooks (in English or L1): 3 words they used today; 2 things they did well; 1 thing they want to do better or remember for next lesson. They show and explain to the teacher as they leave the classroom.	S S-T

> **Lesson plan Part C**
> ***10:** _____
> How did the students perform and behave in the lesson?
> Were they able to participate in the activity in English?
> Did they achieve the learning outcomes?
> What can I do differently next time? How?

REFLECTION

 First, reflect on the plan you saw in the previous activity. Answer the questions in A. Then think about your own lesson planning and answer the questions in B.

A: The sample lesson plan

Imagine you would like to use the lesson plan in the previous activity with a group of learners in your teaching context. Learners in your context may have different needs relating to their age, context and interests.

1 How easy to follow is the plan for you?
2 How suitable is the plan, including the procedure, for learners in your teaching context?
3 What changes would you make to the plan if you used it with learners in your context?

B: Your planning

1 Until now, how have you planned your lessons? What did you write on your plans? If you are not a practising YL teacher, what have you been shown, have used in teaching practice or would include?
2 How do/would you like to use your lesson plan (e.g. during the class, as a checklist to keep you on track; as a tool for reflection on your practice; as a document for future planning or accountability)?
3 What changes would you now like to make to your lesson planning? Why?

DISCOVERY ACTIVITY

 Look at the collaborative discovery activity. Follow the steps to develop an effective lesson plan template for use in your teaching context. If you are not a practising YL teacher, you could collaborate with a teaching colleague who has young learner classes as they do the activity.

Work with a colleague, if possible:
1 Review this unit and make a list of lesson plan headings and other elements to consider when lesson planning. Decide which are important to include in your teaching context.

2 Devise a lesson plan template which requires the information you have identified as important.

3 Together or individually, plan a short series of lessons using the lesson plan template.

4 Teach the lessons and reflect on the effectiveness and efficiency of the planning process.

5 Meet your colleague again to reflect and discuss the planning process together. Focus on both the effectiveness of the planning in relation to teaching and learning, and on the efficiency of the planning in terms of focusing on the aspects which are important in your context.

6 Revise the lesson plan template, if necessary, so that it better meets your needs.

7 Continue using the template for some time, e.g. a term or more, then meet again to discuss further and reflect on the impact of your detailed planning:

- *Is it useful as a practical tool (including its efficiency in relation to the focus and the amount of time you have for planning)?*
- *Does it make you feel more confident in the classroom?*
- *Have you noticed an improvement in your classroom practice?*
- *Have you noticed any change in your learners' engagement or progress in learning?*
- *Have you used it for accountability? (e.g. shared with parents/caregivers)*

■ TKT: YL Practice task

 Do the practice task for this unit. Time yourself to see how long you take to answer all the questions.
Then check your answers in the answer key on page 158.

For questions **1–6**, match the teacher's planning questions with a heading which relates to the section of the lesson plan which will answer that question, listed **A–G**. There is one extra lesson plan heading which you do not need to use.

Lesson plan headings
A Syllabus fit
B Learning outcomes
C Learning resources
D Possible problems and solutions
E Extension activity
F Assessment evidence
G Lesson evaluation

Teacher's planning questions
1 How will I be able to see how much progress the learners are making in the lesson?
2 What will I need to prepare and take to this lesson?
3 What do I want my learners to learn and take away from the lesson?
4 What might go wrong and how can I avoid it?
5 If some learners have time left after the main activity, what can they do to further their learning?
6 Where does this lesson come in the unit?

Unit 6 Classroom materials: How can I challenge and support children's learning when I select and use classroom materials?

LEARNING OUTCOMES

By the end of this unit, you will...
KNOWLEDGE: know how to analyse materials for suitability to a group of children
SKILLS: be able to find appropriate solutions to common problems with classroom materials

■ Starter Question

Before you begin this unit, read the starter question and make some notes. Then read the commentary and compare it to your notes.

 What kinds of materials are you familiar with, or are available in your teaching context?

COMMENTARY

Learning materials are 'anything which is used specifically with the intention of increasing pupils' knowledge and experience of the language' (Moon, 2000, p. 86); they come in many forms and use different media. They may be developed for language teaching and learning, or they may be designed for 'real' purposes. They are often tied to a ***curriculum*** or course ***syllabus***, depending on the teaching ***context***, but they may also be additional resources (see Unit 7).

Print-based teaching and learning materials
Courses often follow a ***coursebook*** (sometimes known as 'textbook'), which may include different components such as a Student's Book and Workbook for the children to use, a Teacher's Book, which supports the teacher in lesson planning, and other multimedia resources such as classroom audio (e.g. on a CD or as web-based audio files), video (e.g. on a DVD, as web-based media files or streamed) and other web-based ***resources*** which children can use online or which teachers can download and print to use as ***handouts***, ***flashcards*** or classroom posters to manage their classes. These kinds of coursebook packages can help a teacher provide a range of different language ***input*** and ***practice*** activities in a coherent way.

Teachers may also turn to sets of printed photocopiable resources, often for ***supplementary materials***, which can be in the form of handouts, complete lessons or sequences of lessons. An example is *'Primary Communication Box'* and others in this series of photocopiable resources for primary ELT from Cambridge University Press & Assessment.

Often these kinds of print-based materials are developed for a global market. They are usually written and produced by experienced teachers and writers, and are generally very appealing visually and of high quality. However, they may not fully meet the needs of specific children or contexts, so may need adjusting, as we will see later in this unit.

Stories, picturebooks and readers

Many young learner coursebooks include short stories within the units or as additional components. As additional resources, teachers may also find and use **picturebooks** written for English language learners, such as *a graded reader*, or for English-speaking children. They might be printed or digital, and some printed books come in a large format (**big books**), so they can be used easily with a whole class.

Stories are an excellent support for language learning and can really motivate children. It can sometimes be challenging to find a story which suits the age and language level and needs of your students, however. We may choose to read a story aloud and make minor changes to the language if necessary, or to *pre-teach* key words to make it more accessible.

Audio-visual materials

These may be on a CD or DVD, or they could be sound or video files downloadable or streamed online. Again, they may be developed for use with a particular course, for English language learners or fluent English speakers. These materials bring a range of different voices and characters into the classroom. If a recording is very challenging, it can be supported by showing some or all of the *transcript*, or by focusing on understanding main ideas rather than specific detail. It can be difficult to re-make professionally made recordings.

■ Key concepts

> Reflect on the *key concept* question. Brainstorm your ideas, then expand your notes as you read.
>
> *What do you think about when deciding which classroom materials to use in your lessons?* **List three or four points.**

COMMENTARY

Materials are an important element in teaching and learning because they are a visual or audio source of language input and support, but they need to be used effectively in order to motivate learners and provide them with what they need to learn. Often, courses follow a coursebook which has been chosen by an institution or school, although many teachers are allowed to use it flexibly. Some teachers may decide to create all their own materials, but this can be very time-consuming and expensive, and requires the teacher to have a strong understanding of the principles of materials and course design for young learners, as it requires a specific skillset. This includes skills in developing a coherent set of well-produced, age-appropriate materials which will motivate children and support language growth and development over time. In some teaching contexts, teachers are required to follow a prescribed coursebook which follows a curriculum or syllabus, often prescribed at a national level by an Education Ministry, with lessons already planned for them. At the other extreme, some teachers may need to decide on all their materials themselves which will help the children in their class work towards specified course, syllabus or curriculum *objectives*. In other cases, children may make or find the materials themselves. In most cases, teachers use a range of materials, and therefore need to make regular decisions about materials when they plan and deliver lessons: what to use, when to use it and how to modify or *supplement* it.

Learner needs

As we saw in Part 1, every learning context and every child is unique. This means that different learners have different needs. When teachers choose materials, they may think about the following key questions, among others, to decide how suitable materials are for their lesson:

Language and skills	Is the level of language at and slightly above my learners' level? Is the language *authentic*, useful and contextualised? Is there an appropriate balance of (or focus on) listening, speaking, reading and writing? Is there a focus on non-language skills and strategies (e.g. cognitive strategies, learning strategies)?
Content	Is the content interesting and relevant to my learners' lives? Is the content at the right level of maturity for my learners? Is the content culturally appropriate for my learners?
Practice activities and tasks	Is there a variety of tasks and activities? Are the tasks and activities *communicative*? Is there a variety of *interaction patterns*? Do the tasks and activities stimulate 21st century skills? Are the tasks and activities fun and motivational? Is there opportunity for *personalisation*?

Physical attributes

We also need to consider the quality and availability of materials:

Quality	Are the materials accurate (e.g. give accurate *models* of language)? Are the instructions clear and supported with pictures, icons, models or examples? Are the materials well presented and appealing to the age group?
Availability	Do I need access to printed copies? If so, how much do they cost? Are the materials copyright free, photocopiable or downloadable? Do I have access to the right equipment to use the materials (e.g. teacher or student device, projector and/or *interactive whiteboard*)?

We can see, then, that selecting materials in lesson planning can require thought, care and attention.

Key concepts and the YL classroom

> Reflect on the *key concepts and the YL classroom* question. Brainstorm your ideas, then expand your notes as you read.
>
> *What kinds of problems do you or other teachers sometimes have with materials?* **Think of two or three problems and some possible solutions.**

COMMENTARY

Teachers often need to adapt materials if they don't meet some of the key criteria noted above, which is quite often the case. This is the case for coursebooks as well as material teachers may source from other resource books, authentic materials, materials from the internet or those shared by colleagues.

We learned in Part 1 of *The TKT Course: YL Module* that we should **scaffold** learning, that is actively help and support children so that they can learn to their own potential. Often the material may need to be changed to provide your class or individual children with either *support* – help and assistance when the material or a part of it is too difficult or outside of the children's experience – or *challenge* – an additional push when the material or part of it is too simple in its language, cognitive demand or content for some or all of the children in the class.

There are numerous ways in which teachers might change material in order to make it more suitable for the children in the class:

Adapt – make changes to the material
For example:
- You may rewrite a written text to add, simplify or remove detail or language; if it is too long, break it into parts for a **jigsaw** task or shorten it.
- You may modify a task. We can help learners with a difficult reading or listening text by providing a simplified task. Similarly, we can add challenge to a task if the reading or listening text is quite simple. You can do this by, for example, adjusting the level of cognitive challenge (making the task simpler in the kind of thinking it involves), or by changing the skill focus to one which your students prefer or need more practice in, e.g. they write something instead of saying it, or the other way around. You could change an activity to make it more interactive, or to one where children **collaborate** on a group task, rather than work alone or alongside each other.
- You may decide to change the skill focus – for a class with low level **literacy** skills, learners may achieve a task more easily if it is spoken rather than written, or they may benefit from hearing a text while following the words in a written version with their finger.
- You may want to change an activity so that it is more child-friendly or better suited to the cultural background of your learners, for example: *Hangman* could be adapted so it involves stepping stones leading up to a house; '*What's the time, Mr. Wolf?*' might have Mr. Wolf as a bee, trying to get pollen from the flowers (the other children).

Add – provide something in addition to the material

For example:

- You could add an initial stage for **brainstorming** ideas or to support children with key vocabulary, concepts or skills.
- You may wish to provide more visual support or examples using flashcards or **realia** to help children understand ideas and vocabulary, particularly if this helps children relate learning to their own life. To provide support with a challenging or complicated task, use prompts, models and examples. These could be written on the materials themselves or could be included when giving instructions.
- A further addition to support children could be a **word bank**, a glossary or a mini dictionary, which learners can refer to as they read or listen or use when they do a speaking or writing task. It might be on the page, on a separate handout, or could be something learners create themselves. A word bank might include words and phrases you have brainstormed with learners and put on the board.
- You may want to add an opportunity for personalisation, which will help learners make meaningful connections with their classroom learning, such as extending a food quiz activity to include guessing which foods other learners like or don't like, or encouraging learners to compare something in a text with their own experiences.
- **Extension activities** may be useful for additional practice in a language skill which your learners particularly need to review or develop, or you could extend a project by adding an extra research task.

Omit – take something out

For example:

- You may want to remove or skip something in the material where, for example, there is too much on the page or too many activities for your lesson.
- Alternatively, you may feel that your class don't really need to practise a particular skill or vocabulary if you feel they have already acquired the language. Sometimes, however, these tasks could be set as **at-home tasks** or be used in review lessons.
- You may rewrite materials, omitting some language which is too far above children's level, or is inappropriate for them, or you may remove words, phrases or sentences if a text is too long.
- Similarly, if images or ideas are culturally or age sensitive, they should probably be removed.

Reject – decide not to use the material

You may decide that the material is too difficult to change or is completely inappropriate or unnecessary in the time you have, in which case you may reject it altogether.

As coursebooks are designed to build understanding and learning across the units, concepts are often returned to and built upon in later learning. When modifying course material, we may look backwards in a course to see what is missing or has not been covered or reviewed enough for our learners. It is also important, however, to look forwards in the course to make sure we are not taking out something that features again later as assumed knowledge. This could be vocabulary or language needed in a later activity, lesson or unit, but may also sometimes be part of a story line involving coursebook characters or a two-part project or task.

Exploring the concepts in practice

FOLLOW-UP ACTIVITY *(see page 151 for answers)*

 Look at the extracts and material below. Read the teacher's comments and question. What advice would you give to each teacher? Make a note of your answers.

1.

Extract from Nixon and Tomlinson (2017) *Power Up,* Level 2, p. 7: Cambridge University Press & Assessment

The teacher says:

'We are starting a new unit in the coursebook. It begins with vocabulary and a ***chant***, which the class listen and respond to.

Many of these words are new to my students, though, and they may have difficulty relating to some of them because of their home environment (e.g. field, lake or forest). Our community is in a very hot, dry, desert climate, which is very different from the picture.

What could I do to make the material clearer and more relevant to my learners?'

2.

Extract from Alarcón, Domínguez and Quesada (2019) *Science Skills* Level 1, p. 47: Cambridge University Press & Assessment

The teacher says:

'My class is learning about life cycles in other subjects, so I would like to build on this topic in English. I like the project in this material because it is activity-based and helps to develop cognitive and learning strategies. The instructions in the project use difficult language, however, and I don't think the pictures are enough to help my learners understand what to do.

What advice would you give me so I can use this fun activity?'

Arrange to meet other teachers in your institution, school or context, if possible. Alternatively, you could meet online or do this task on a teachers' forum with teachers in another context. Do step 1 of the task to prepare for Step 2, the meeting.

Step 1:

Look through a coursebook you know well or would like to use. Using the mind map template, note positive points about the coursebook in green and negatives in red, at least one for each category. You can add more categories if you wish.

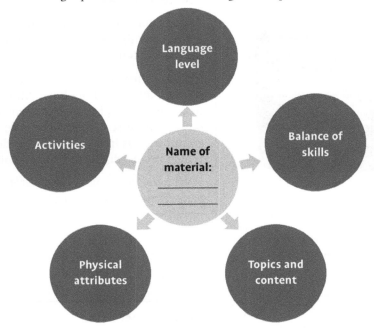

Step 2:

Meet with the other teachers. Share your views about the coursebook you evaluated. Listen to their opinions of the coursebooks they chose and discuss ways they improve their coursebooks to suit their learners.

DISCOVERY ACTIVITY

 Follow the steps for investigating your use of learning materials.

Planning
- Look through an upcoming unit or sequence of materials you plan to use with your class. This could be the same material you had in mind in the reflection activity in this unit.
- Answer the questions outlined in the Key concepts section in this unit.
- Based on your answers to these questions, decide what you will do with the materials so that they better meet the needs of your class. Will you *adapt* them in some way? *Add* something to them? Take something out *(omit)*?
- Make the changes to your materials.

Teaching
- Plan and deliver your lesson(s) using these materials. As you deliver the lesson(s), *observe* the children to see how they respond to the materials. *Monitor* so you can watch and listen to them as they do the tasks. You could collect some of their written work, if included.

Evaluating and reflecting
- During and after the lesson(s), ask the children's opinions on the materials and note their answers. Children of all ages can give you useful feedback on materials if you ask specific questions. You could ask them what they liked and didn't like about the materials, and whether they found them clear and easy to follow or understand. Older children in the 6–12 age range may also be able to say how effective for learning they were and/or what they would like to see more or less of in the materials.
- Review your notes and samples of work. To what extent did the changes you made to the materials improve teaching and learning? What can you do to further improve the materials?

You can use your TKT: YL PD Journal to record and keep track of this investigation. Remember to follow any ethical procedures required by your institution and to ensure you have informed consent of your learners and other participants before collecting any classroom data.

■ TKT: YL Practice task

 Do the practice task for this unit. Time yourself to see how long you take to answer all the questions.
Then check your answers in the answer key on page 158.

For questions **1–6**, read the teacher's comment about a decision they made about their use of materials. Choose the correct description listed **A–C**.

1 **Teacher's comment:**
'I found a great song to use with my class, which matches the topic and vocabulary we are learning perfectly. I want the children to try to sing along after hearing it and doing some miming activities, but it is very fast! It's difficult to simplify a song, so I'm going to ask students to listen for just a few words and phrases, then mime and sing those.'

The teacher plans to:

A   Adapt the song

B   Provide a simple task

C   Omit the song

2 Teacher's comment:

The current unit is about fruit and vegetables. There is a text in the unit about healthy eating which includes some vegetables my children have never seen in real life. I think I will look online and find some pictures to show students so they can see what these vegetables look like and talk a bit about them.

The teacher plans to:

A   Add some visual support

B   Adapt the text

C   Simplify the topic

3 Teacher's comment:

I found a storybook on the same topic as our unit. However, it's written for English-speaking children, and some of the language is quite difficult. I noticed that a few of these unknown words are key in understanding the story, but other vocabulary isn't. I'm going to prepare some pictures to show learners before reading the story to introduce them to these words. Then they'll understand the story better.

The teacher plans to:

A   Pre-teach vocabulary

B   Personalise content

C   Rewrite the story

4 Teacher's comment:

There is a really valuable task in the coursebook that I would like to use in class. However, the instructions are quite complicated as the task has several stages, and I don't think the children will understand what to do. I've broken down the instructions into steps and put them on a separate worksheet. I've added some pictures to show learners what's expected of them at each step.

The teacher plans to:

A   Personalise the activity

B   Provide examples

C   Simplify the task by omitting steps

5 Teacher's comment:

The children want to play some online vocabulary practice games related to the topic. I previewed the game: It looks fun and will help them practise the topic words, but there are some words in it that we haven't covered in the class material. I'll prepare a glossary, which learners can check if they need to.

The teacher plans to:

A   Provide an example

B   Add written instructions

C   Add support

6 **Teacher's comment:**

Some children in my class are at an early stage of literacy development; their listening and speaking skills are stronger. There is a writing activity in the coursebook where children should write sentences about their family. I think this would be useful practice for them, but these children are not usually able to write sentences independently, so I have added a stage to my lesson where we will work together to write example sentences on the board. I'll leave these on the board so that the learners can refer to them if they need to.

The teacher plans to:

A   Provide model sentences

B   Add a transcript

C   Personalise the content

Unit 7   Additional classroom resources: How can I select, adapt and supplement classroom resources?

LEARNING OUTCOMES

By the end of this unit, you will…
KNOWLEDGE: know when and what kinds of additional resources teachers may plan for to enrich teaching and learning
SKILLS: be able to choose appropriate additional resources for a specific teaching context or moment

■ Starter Question

Before you begin this unit, read the starter questions and make some notes. Then read the commentary and compare it to your notes.

 What do you understand by the term 'additional resources'? Why use them in YL lessons? Write a definition and think of at least two reasons for using them.

COMMENTARY

Additional *resources* are, simply, learning resources that teachers use in addition to their course material. We sometimes see the equivalent term '*supplementary* resources'. The range of resources teachers might use to *supplement* their course material is almost limitless, but often they may use *realia*, *flashcards*, songs, video and so on. We will look at examples in more detail in the next section.

We saw in Unit 6 that course material often needs adapting and supplementing in order to make it more appropriate for our own learners. This may help us to:

- engage learners, gain and keep their attention through active participation.
- add interest, creativity, fun or physical activity to our lessons by balancing sitting time with moving time (*stirrers* and *settlers*).
- add extra language or vocabulary *practice activities*.
- provide language practice in a different way, using (a) different skill(s).
- support understanding of topic, language or vocabulary.
- extend learning of language or vocabulary, for example using the language in a different context, or adding some vocabulary items, perhaps those which are especially relevant to our own learners.
- extend learning of content or align it with the *curriculum* (i.e. add a **cross-curricular** element).

Above all, additional resources can help develop the **whole child**, because they can stimulate children in different ways and help develop a wider range of skills than those supported in the course material, including 21st century skills, in particular the '4Cs': critical thinking, communication, collaboration and creativity.

Key concepts

> Reflect on the *key concept* question. Brainstorm your ideas, then expand your notes as you read.
>
> *Look at the purposes for additional resources listed in the previous section. What kinds of resources could / do you use for these purposes?* **Note resources suitable for three or four of these purposes.**

COMMENTARY

Additional resources can be made specifically for children (or any learners) learning English, for more general classroom use, or they can be authentic, that is materials which are designed for real-world use but have been borrowed to use for language learning, for example:

- *Printed materials from outside the classroom:* menus, greetings cards, maps, photographs, etc.
- *Printed materials for English-speaking children:* **picturebooks** (and supporting resources, such as finger **puppets**, toys, *props*), comics, etc.
- *Rhymes, songs and **chants**:* These may be borrowed from published collections or be well-known (often available online as audio or with video clips). Teachers also write rhymes themselves sometimes.

- *Children's games:* word puzzles (e.g. wordsearches, crosswords), common **playground** or classroom or playground games (e.g. hopscotch), memory games (e.g. '**Pelmanism'**, '**Kim's Game'**), etc.
- *Toys:* Toy vehicles, fruit, animals, etc., finger and hand puppets, masks, dolls and teddies, etc.
- *Art and craft materials:* These involve learners using resources to design and make things, such as mini books, origami, masks, puppets, greetings cards, collages, etc.
- *Other realia:* Real objects, such as clothes, food packaging, objects of different colours, shapes etc.

Authentic materials can be very stimulating. They often provide a familiar, real-world ***context*** for language, drawing language away from the ***coursebook*** and into a real-world use which is familiar to children in their daily lives. They can be used to demonstrate meaning clearly, to connect topics, vocabulary and language to children's understanding of the world. Some language used in published resources (e.g. brochures, stories, songs) may be above-level, however, so it is important to make a related task achievable, based on the language the learners are capable of, and focus attention on parts of the text they can largely understand. Learners can be very motivated by the sense of achievement at understanding or using something authentic in English, and will enjoy doing so.

Non-authentic resources, that is resources made specifically for use in the classroom, are also often stimulating; they are designed to meet the classroom needs directly, often relate specifically to the course material, and can be photocopied or easily used with children.

We may use resources which are commercially produced, teacher-made, or they may be learner- or class-made. Let's look at how teachers might use different kinds of authentic and non-authentic material in the language classroom:

Visual learning resources

As we saw in Part 1, children learn in many different ways, and children's cognition is often stimulated or supported by visuals, which can help them understand and remember concepts, language and vocabulary, and relate the ideas to their own understanding or knowledge of the world. We can use different kinds of visuals to help show the meaning of vocabulary or language clearly, to let children associate or read words

connected to images, and to show how things are related, such as in size, category or meaning. To do this, we may use teacher flashcards and pictures, sets of flashcards for learners to manipulate or play games, posters for children to refer to or use in an activity.

Often these kinds of resources come as components with coursebook packages and match the course material. However, learners themselves can create their own sets of flashcards, which gives them extra practice and is sometimes more engaging and meaningful to them. Learners can create and use their own drawings, paintings and crafts in the classroom, which can then be used as visual resources.

Many children enjoy watching films, TV and short video clips. We can use this kind of visual to present or review a language point or vocabulary, for storytelling, or songs. Children could act out scenes, guess, imagine or create scripts, lyrics or short dialogues. Groups or whole classes can easily create their own video clips or shorts, which can encourage them to work to the best of their ability and take pride in their work.

Comics and graphic novels are authentic and visually appealing. They are popular among children and can stimulate creativity and thinking. They can be adapted for **productive** skills practice, for example writing alternative speech or acting out scenes.

Multi-sensory resources

Multi-sensory learning is where learning activities are designed which stimulate more than one sense at the same time or in a sequence. This supports understanding and memory, connects classroom learning to real life, and can be fun and motivational for all learners, while helping children to use and develop different ways of learning. We can often use realia or sometimes ICT for multi-sensory learning, for example, which children can see, hear, touch, smell and taste (Note that it is essential that parental/caregiver consent is given, in case of allergy or health issues). We can also use resources such as small dishes of sand, modelling clay and objects we find in nature. These can be manipulated by children to represent letters and words, or used in collages or to represent props, characters or events in a story in a post-story activity. Sound files are easily found online and can be used to represent or portray specific items, moods, actions and so on.

Art and craft resources

Art and craft activities and their resources can be used in the classroom for a wide range of purposes. Children may need to listen to or read instructions as they create origami animals, stimulate their curiosity about nature as they size-order sticks or stones, make and play puzzles, do simple science experiments and so on. These activities may be a part of a ***project***; they may require children to use cognitive strategies (e.g. to ***predict outcome***), to work collaboratively (e.g. through joint planning or presentation) or to learn cross-curricular content (e.g. to learn about colour or perspective).

Digital and web-based resources (ICT or Information and Communication Technology)

There are more and more teaching and learning materials and resources available online or offline which are specifically for language learners, including app-based games children can play using a hand-held device or computer, and other digital resources which come as part of a coursebook package (see, for example, the language learning game for mobile and other language-based games and activities for children.

In addition to such games, there is such a wealth of downloadable, printable ***worksheets*** and materials such as pictures, flashcards and games available online, that it can be quite an overwhelming choice. Often, this kind of material has been made for another specific group of learners or may contain inappropriate or learners or may contain inappropriate or even inaccurate language or content. It is very important, therefore, to check any web-sourced materials very carefully before use and to be ready to adapt them for your learners if necessary.

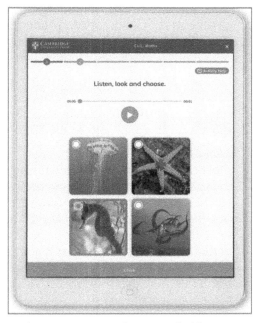

Figure 1: *Guess What!*, Cambridge University Press & Assessment

Video material is also readily available online, including songs, short video clips and animations. These can supplement a coursebook or *syllabus* by presenting or giving extra practice of vocabulary or language in a stimulating way; songs and music can help us incorporate physical activity in our lessons, through dancing and showing understanding through *gestures* and mime. As mentioned above, children may make their own videos, which could be shared on a password-protected space online.

Older children can be directed to the internet to find out information and research a topic, for a project or a task such as a group presentation, poster or writing task. When children use any web-based resources, it is essential that they are sent to the resource or a child-friendly search engine directly, or that a child internet safety control service is in use which will ensure safety online by, for example, preventing learners from accessing inappropriate sites and pages sharing personal information or details, or interacting with unknown people online. Before you use the internet with your learners, or as part of a classroom rule-writing activity at the beginning of the year, negotiate and write guidelines for safe internet use with your learners. They may be related to searching or sharing information, staying on task (e.g. keeping only relevant pages, sites, tabs or apps open); you may also wish to address concerns such as identifying fake news, critical reading and appropriate use of web-based sources.

People

Teachers and learners are resources in themselves – free and always available, too! We can use our bodies in *TPR (Total Physical Response)* activities, miming, action rhymes and songs, and drama-based activities, for example. Using physical exercise, dance, yoga, meditation and mindfulness training activities can support children's emotional needs and development and promote physical and mental health. This could be part of a *routine* at a particular point in a lesson, as a stirrer to break up a desk-based activity or as a physical response to new language.

Learners are often very interested to know more about their teacher, and your own anecdotes, stories, personal photos and experiences can be a motivating learning resource. Learners of all ages also have their own experiences, stories and ideas to share, and these too can be used as a resource.

The classroom

Most classrooms have their own resources already available to teachers. The board (blackboard, whiteboard or *interactive whiteboard*) for example can be used by the teacher and also by the children, who can write or draw on it to show understanding or explain something. It can also be used for whole-class activities, team games and so on. Different coloured chalk or pens are very useful. Classrooms often have a screen with a data projector, to show a computer screen, and some may be equipped with interactive whiteboards. In both cases, children can interact with these as learning resources, help demonstrate activities, take part in online games, deliver mini presentations and so on.

Teachers may also be allowed to use a **display board** or to decorate the classroom in other ways. Learners may choose to display some work, create a topic-based display, put up posters with useful classroom language, negotiated classroom rules, banks of 'tricky words and phrases' and so on. By adding labels and other written words around the classroom, children will regularly see words, so will remember them more easily from this **print-rich environment**.

■ Key concepts and the YL classroom

Reflect on the *key concepts and the YL classroom* question. Brainstorm your ideas, then expand your notes as you read.

 How might additional resources and props, such as toys, games, puppets, class mascots, music or routines be used differently for younger and older children in the 6–12 age range? **Brainstorm your ideas for one or two resource types.**

COMMENTARY

We saw in Unit 1 that there are some differences between older and younger children in the 6–12 age range. These include cognitive, physical, social-emotional and other needs and characteristics. They also include what is familiar and enjoyable to them. When considering additional resources, the question of age-appropriacy is important, as children often have strong preferences for or against particular types if intended for younger or older children.

Toys: Younger children are more likely to see toys as something they play with regularly and will be motivated as a result. Older children, on the other hand, may feel they are only for little children. While we may use toys often with younger children as visual or physical resources in different activities, we may need to be more selective and choose age-appropriate toys as props or characters for **drama**, ***dialogues*** and other animation tasks, or perhaps to demonstrate meaning.

Games: Older children may find word games, ***problem-solving*** games and games with more complex rules stimulating and fun, for example board games, crossword puzzles, ***role-playing*** games and online games. Simpler, more visual games, which can be easily explained and demonstrated, and are less complex in their gameplay, are usually more suitable for younger children. They may involve fewer or no written words and may be more physical. Children of all ages can play games in the playground, although these may also differ depending on the age group.

Puppets and mascots: Typically, teachers of younger learners may use a class puppet to help manage the classroom, to ***model*** language, to carry out routines and allow children to use or speak directly with the puppet to help and encourage them speak, especially if they are a little shy. The class puppet is a character with his/her own name, personality and background, and often only speaks and understands English. Older children may respond better to a class mascot which is like a class supporter, than a puppet and are less likely to want to interact with it directly; however, a mascot can also serve as a sounding board for ideas or a friendly listening ear for children who wish to talk in private to someone. Children can make their own puppets and mascots, as well as masks, which can also help some children feel more confident, whatever their age.

Music: Music can be used effectively in many different ways, such as in the background for calming effect, for singing along to, for dancing to, for doing actions and mimes or even for meditation and relaxation times. Children generally enjoy singing along or dancing to music at any age, although younger children may be less inhibited. A positive, uninhibited model by the teacher is likely to motivate and inspire older children to sing and move to music, or a teacher may decide to use more chants and fewer songs with older children. Similarly, younger children usually engage quickly with dancing and physical responses, whereas older children may need extra *motivation* or prefer responding verbally to music.

Routines: Unit 1 introduced the benefits of *routines* in the classroom: these are a resource in themselves and can make use of other kinds of physical additional resources, such as calendars, registers, interactive mood or weather wall charts. Routines often also involve songs, chants and movement, especially with younger children. They are, however, suitable for any age group, but may differ in their use of resources and the language used by both teacher and learners. For example, younger children may sing a goodbye song at the end of the lesson or hold up a smiley face card to show how well they remember vocabulary or target language in a lesson, while older children may be asked to complete **exit tickets** as part of a closing routine, where they reflect more on their learning.

■ Exploring the concepts in practice

FOLLOW-UP ACTIVITY *(see page 151 for answers)*

 Some teachers are asking for advice. First, read the teachers' questions and think what your response would be. Then, match two possible responses with each request. Could any of these ideas be useful in your teaching context?

Teacher 1: I'm planning to introduce numbers 1–10 with my beginner class of 6–7-year-olds. I'm looking for a fun, active way to practise counting. What additional resources would you recommend?

Teacher 2: In the new coursebook unit, my upper primary learners will learn food-related vocabulary for a healthy-eating topic. I wanted to play a flashcard game to help them remember the words, but I don't have any of the right flashcards. What can I do?

Teacher 3: My 7–9-year-olds' class is really enjoying the animals topic in the coursebook, so I would like to extend it. They love all kinds of songs, storybooks, comics, cartoons and so on. Do you have any recommendations?

Teacher 4: I found some kids' brochures about famous places to visit in Italy – they are for English speakers. There's quite a lot of difficult vocabulary and sentences, but I think they would motivate my learners in the travel unit. What can I do?

"
Teacher 5: I noticed that several learners have problems spelling some basic words. How could I use additional resources to provide extra practice for them in a fun way?
"

"
Teacher 6: I asked the children to bring some old magazines from home. I want them to find some pictures and words related to the topic we are looking at, but I don't know what to ask them to do. Can you suggest something?
"

A: You could ask learners to work in *pairs*. They play a guessing game – one learner turns around; their partner traces the letters of a word on their back with their finger. They should guess which word is being spelled.	**B:** They could cut out the pictures and, in pairs, use them to describe a scene or a story by sticking them to paper.
C: You could give animal story starter prompts (e.g. using story flashcards). Children create their own simple story, then write and draw a cartoon using a template.	**D**: You could ask children to bring some food packaging from home. They could cut this up and stick it to card to make their own flashcards. Then they can use the flashcards to play a game such as *Happy Families* or a ranking activity, putting them in order from most healthy to least healthy.
E: You could ask children to draw their own flashcards. They could write word cards to go with them, then play **pelmanism**, where all cards are placed face-down; learners take it in turns to turn over two cards to find matching pairs.	**F:** You could play a game with giant dice where children guess or predict what number they will throw (you will need to teach up to 12 though!).
G: You could bring in some modelling clay or toy letters. Play a game where children should spell a word correctly using the clay or letters. They could play this game in small groups. It could be a competition or it could be *collaborative*.	**H:** They could play a guessing game in small groups. After cutting out three or four pictures each, they put them together in the middle of the table. They play a *20 questions* game to guess which picture a learner has chosen (the group can ask up to 20 yes/no questions to discover which picture the player are thinking of).

I: You could *pre-teach* some of the vocabulary which is useful to your learners and specific to a place (e.g. *cathedral* or *Roman*). Then set a simple *scanning* task – first ask them to predict which place description will contain these words. They can then look through the text to find out if they predicted correctly.	**J:** You could bring in a storybook to read with them, such as *The Tiger Who Came to Tea* or *Going on a Bear Hunt*.
K: You could focus children's attention on the pictures and on sections which are easier to understand as they look at the material.	**L:** You could use a counting song, like *Ten Green Bottles* or *10 Little Ducks*. Children could hold up flashcards, toy ducks or bottles with numbers on when they hear the numbers, then practise singing the song.

REFLECTION

 Brainstorm and list different additional resources. Evaluate them for use in your teaching context, or a context you know well. Make notes using a chart similar to the one below. You could copy it into your TKT: YL PD Journal.

Additional resource	Age appropriacy	How it could be used	How these learners might react to it	Possible problems	Where/how to find it
Puppet					
Food realia					
Web-based vocabulary games					

DISCOVERY ACTIVITY

 Write and conduct a survey to find out about the kinds of additional resources your colleagues or other teachers in your network use in their lessons. Share the findings with these teachers.

Step 1: Think about what you would like to find out from other teachers, for example:

- The kinds of additional resources they use frequently in their teaching
- The kinds of activities the learners do with these resources
- How they supplement the coursebook or other course material
- Where they get the resources from
- Which age group, topic, language etc. they are useful for
- The kinds of problems they have experienced with additional resources in the classroom
- How they solved these problems

Step 2: Write a short questionnaire to survey the teachers. It should take no more than 5–10 minutes to complete. It could be in English or in another shared language.

Step 3: Conduct the survey with teachers in your school or network. You could use paper, email or a web-based surveying tool.

Step 4: Look at and analyse the findings and put together a short report.

Step 5: Share the report with the teachers. You could do this in a meeting and then talk more about this topic.

■ TKT: YL Practice task

 Do the practice task for this unit. Time yourself to see how long you take to answer all the questions.

Then check your answers in the answer key on page 158.

For questions **1–6**, what kind of additional resource are these teachers talking about? Match the teacher's comments **1–6** with the additional resource type **A–F**.

Additional resources

A	Realia
B	Art and craft materials and activities
C	Puppets
D	Learner-generated video clips
E	Flashcards
F	ICT

Teacher's comments

1 'I'm going to supplement the coursebook material with a creative group project using items children found on a trip to the park.'

2 'The children each brought one old (clean!) sock to class. I'm hoping to use them for storytelling.'

3 'I want the children to review vocabulary (meaning and spelling of words) by playing a game in pairs, where they match pictures and words.'

4 'The children have prepared and learned role-play dialogues. They are going to record them so that others can watch.'

5 'The children are learning colour words, so I'm looking for things in my classroom to use for a colour categorisation activity.'

6 'I've found a fun app where children take part in a learning adventure as a character, answering questions and solving problems.'

Reflection on learning in Part 2

Well done, you have completed Part 2. This part of *The TKT Course: Young Learner Module* aimed to extend your understanding and skills in planning and preparing lessons for young learners, and in analysing, selecting, adapting and modifying materials and resources for learning. This part also developed your knowledge and skills in preparation for the second part of the TKT: YL Module test: *Planning and preparing young learner lessons.*

Look back to the introduction to this part of the book. There, you assessed your understanding before beginning the unit. Re-assess your understanding in each area.

You also wrote some questions or identified areas to find out more about in each unit. How well do you think you have achieved these? What can you do to better achieve those you need to work on? For example:
- Re-read a section of the unit(s).
- Re-do or do more exploration activities (Second C of each unit).
- Discuss the unit(s) content with other teachers in your school or network.
- Re-do the TKT: YL practice task(s).
- Look in the *TKT glossary* or the glossary in this book to check meanings of key terms and concepts you are unsure about.
- Reflect on your classroom teaching more closely.
- Look for other readings or resources on the topic(s).

Write yourself two or three objectives for further learning and development in your TKT: YL PD Journal.

■ References and further recommended reading

PART 2 REFERENCES

Moon, J. (2000). *Children Learning English.* Oxford: Macmillan.

Nixon, C. and Tomlinson, M. (2018). *Power Up.* Pupil's Book. (New Ed.), Level 2. Cambridge: Cambridge University Press & Assessment.

Science Skills Level 1, Pupil's Book. Cambridge: Cambridge University Press & Assessment.

RECOMMENDED FURTHER READING

Arnold, W. and Rixon, S. (2008). Materials for Teaching English to Young Learners. In B. Tomlinson, *English Language Learning Materials. A Critical View.* London: Continuum.

Bland, J. (2023). *Compelling Stories for English Language Learners.* London: Bloomsbury.

Dobbs, J. (2001). *Using the Board in the Language Classroom.* Cambridge: Cambridge University Press & Assessment.

Garton, S. and Copland, F. (Eds.) (2019). *The Routledge Handbook of Teaching English to Young Learners.* (Part 4 – Technology and Young Learner Curriculum). London: Routledge.

Pinter, A. (2006). *Teaching Young Language Learners.* Oxford: Oxford University Press. (Chapter 9).

Shin, J. K., Savić, V. and Machida, T. (2021). *The 6 Principles for Exemplary Teaching of English Learners.* Alexandria: TESOL International Association. (Chapter 3).

Part 3 | Teaching Young Learners

Introduction to Part 3

Part 3 will help you better understand as well as use strategies and activities to teach and manage a young learner classroom effectively. You will deepen your knowledge about how to scaffold children's understanding and use of language through your own use of language and through strategies you may use in the classroom, then consolidate learning using appropriate practice activities. You will also consider strategies and techniques for managing young learners in class. This part of *The TKT Course: Young Learner Module* will support your knowledge and skills in preparation for the third part of the TKT: YL Module test: *Teaching Young Learners*. You can find more information in the *TKT: YL syllabus* in the module handbook, which is available online.

In the first unit of this part of the book, Unit 8, you'll think about how to support and challenge learners using teacher language and teaching strategies. First, you'll consider the use of the term **scaffolding**, both metaphorically in education and in its real-world use. You'll then reflect on the teacher's role in scaffolding understanding and use of language before looking at strategies a teacher may employ to do this.

Unit 9 looks at practice activities, that is how we can use motivating, effective classroom activities to engage young learners and give them the opportunity to consolidate their language use and understanding through practice in the classroom. You'll consider specific features of effective practice activities and points to keep in mind when planning them, before looking at examples of activities teachers have found effective in YL classrooms.

In Unit 10, we will focus on managing learning in YL classrooms. You will first think about what the term 'classroom management' means, then will consider how teachers can develop a positive classroom atmosphere, which will support children in their learning. Finally in this unit, you'll look at how teachers can be more effective managers of challenging behaviour.

Towards the end of each unit, you will find follow-up activities, which are designed to deepen and extend your thinking in relation to the unit content. These will help you reflect on the classroom application of your learning in your own context. These are followed by a set of TKT: YL practice questions based on the unit theme. It is recommended that you use your TKT: YL PD Journal to keep and organise your notes.

As you did in Parts 1 and 2, look at the *can-do statements* before you begin the units in this part of the book. Evaluate your own understanding and skills for each one. After completing Part 3, return to these and re-assess yourself. From that, you can develop an action plan to continue focusing on any particular areas you feel necessary.

SELF-ASSESSMENT

Unit	Rate yourself from: **1** (*Limited or not at all*) to **5** (*This is a strength*)	Rating before Part 3	Rating after Part 3
8	*I can* identify or select appropriate scaffolding strategies to support children in their learning.		
9	*I can* plan motivating, effective practice activities to help children consolidate language use and understanding.		
10	*I can* choose appropriate strategies to manage children's learning in the classroom.		

In your TKT: YL PD Journal, identify two or three questions or areas you'd like to know more about in each unit in Part 3. When you have finished Part 3, return to these to see if you have answered them. If you haven't, read around the topic using the recommended reading list at the end of this part of the book. You can also find many resources for teacher professional development online.

Unit 8   Supporting children's language: How can I scaffold children's understanding and use of language?

LEARNING OUTCOMES

By the end of this unit, you will…
KNOWLEDGE: know about scaffolding children's learning to support their understanding and use of language in the classroom
SKILLS: be able to identify how teachers use verbal and teaching strategies to support children's language in the classroom

■ Starter Question

Before you begin this unit, read the starter question and make some notes. Then read the commentary and compare it to your notes.

 What do you understand by the word scaffolding – as a teacher or in your own everyday environment?

COMMENTARY

Scaffolding, in everyday speak, is a structure used in construction to help builders access their work or to support a building being constructed or renovated. Scaffolding style, materials and use can differ quite considerably between different places and uses: aluminium and steel poles, wooden planks and a wide range of fixings are common in parts of Europe, while more natural, bamboo scaffolding, constructed in an array of different styles depending on the building, can be found in many parts of Asia. See for example the image of bamboo scaffolding in Hong Kong shown below:

The term *scaffolding* was first used metaphorically by the educational psychologist Jerome Bruner (Cameron, 2001) to refer to the support or assistance given by an adult or more skilled peer to help a child develop from their current level to a higher level, one which is within their potential. This may be development in a skill, knowledge or understanding. In its everyday-life, non-educational meaning, the scaffolding is put in place to support the construction of the building, and it gradually rises or shifts as the construction work progresses, and this function and process is similar in learning and development. Also similar is the idea that scaffolding type, material and form differ between contexts, sometimes quite dramatically, depending on local norm, function and available resources.

Take an example from everyday life: a young child who begins to learn to ride a bicycle. At first, they may use training wheels, or be held firmly by an adult, moving slowly. The training wheels or adult's grip may be gradually loosened as the child begins to balance a little better. Eventually, when the adult thinks the child can balance well enough, they may remove the training wheels or let go altogether. And off the child rides on their bike. The adult is likely to stay with them to help a little more when needed, such as with steering the bike, or their speed, perhaps.

In this example, we can see a skill is being developed. The adult and/or the training wheels provide assistance and support, a scaffold, for the child. This may be physical support but is also likely to be emotional support, with the adult encouraging the child, and giving corrective feedback on the child's skills. As the child improves at the bike-riding skill, the scaffolding is reduced step-by-step, until finally, it is removed altogether. At this point, new scaffolding needs to be put in place, which will support the child to get to the next stage in the skill, and so on. If the scaffolding is inadequate or removed too quickly, the child risks falling off the bike, which can be demoralising and painful. Some children may not want or need as much support, however – perhaps they are more independent or determined, so they try it alone or with a friend's help, not caring about the risks, or they may have used a special pedal-less bike before so can learn to use a pedal bike very quickly. A particularly cautious child, on the other hand, may not want the scaffolding to be removed so soon. Each child differs in the type, intensity and duration of support they need or want, although there is usually a need for some kind of scaffolding by someone who knows more about riding a bike than the child.

■ Key concepts

> Reflect on the *key concept* question. Brainstorm your ideas, then expand your notes as you read.
>
> *What do you think the teacher's role may be in scaffolding in the YL classroom?* **Make a note of two or three ideas.**

COMMENTARY

When we take this metaphor into the classroom, we can see that it is important to give help to children so they can reach a higher level of understanding and production of language. Learning *outcomes* of a lesson describe what the learners can do with language by the end of the lesson that they were not able to do at the beginning. Scaffolding, then, is what teachers (or another more knowledgeable person, including a peer) do to help students achieve those outcomes. Scaffolding also happens at a micro level when we provide help to children so that they understand more in a text, or are able to produce more language in an activity, for example.

There are many different ways we can scaffold children's understanding and use of language, and the teacher can also bring in support from others such as children in the class, family, caregivers or other people in the school or community. Children can also be shown how to provide scaffolding for themselves through the development and use of some of the *learning strategies* we saw in Unit 2.

Here, we will focus on two main types of technique for scaffolding children's understanding and language use:
- *Teacher language* – something the teacher *says* or *writes*.
- *Teaching strategies* – something the teacher *does* or *provides*.

■ Key concepts and the YL classroom

Reflect on the *key concepts and the YL classroom* question. Brainstorm your ideas, then expand your notes as you read.

 How can teachers use language and strategies to support learning in the YL classroom? **Note one or two examples of teacher language and of teaching strategies.**

COMMENTARY

Teacher language
Often without realising, a parent or caregiver may use **parentese** when interacting with their child: language which is slower, more carefully articulated, has a higher pitch, is modified, and often features a lot of repetition and exemplification. The parentese will change as the child grows up and becomes a better user of the language themselves. Adults will continue to modify their language even when speaking to older children in order to make their meaning clear and comprehensible, and also to help the child increase their vocabulary or correct some remaining grammatical mistakes, which are all a normal part of their language development. The same scaffolding tool is commonly used by teachers, usually more deliberately, as they modify the way they use language to meet the needs and level of their students. This is likely to change as the children get older and/or become more proficient in English. Teachers may use their language to scaffold in the following ways:

Graded language is language which is at or near learners' level. When managing learning, activities, interaction, feedback or giving emotional support to a child, for example, the teacher should use language with simple, comprehensible structure and vocabulary, which is delivered deliberately, clearly and at an appropriate pace.

Adjusting language use may involve repeating something or explaining through rephrasing it in different, simpler language.

Questions often serve a scaffolding purpose, to check understanding and guide a child towards understanding or improved language use. These may be **concept check questions** (CCQs), which are simple, **closed questions** to check understanding, or they may be questions which aim to have a child think, to produce a longer, more detailed answer, for example **open** or divergent questions. Giving plenty of **wait time** after asking a question will also help the child organise their thinking and formulate their answer.

Translanguaging is where we use another language to support understanding or use of the second language, here English. This is often a child's **first language (L1)** but may be more than one language in the case of multilingual classrooms, families or communities. This(These) language(s) can be used judiciously by the teacher to support understanding through translation, exemplification or explanation, or it could be used by the child to help express ideas too complex to say in English or support a peer in doing so (mediation).

Correction of learners' spoken language might be done explicitly (for example **finger correction**), through **recast** and **reformulation** (where the teacher provides the correct language, but doesn't draw attention to the mistake), **echo correction** (where the teacher repeats the mistake but uses **intonation** to signal it as a mistake), questions and clarification requests (where the teacher might ask about the language the child has used to encourage them to correct themselves). Alternatively, the teacher may ignore a mistake or decide to deal with it later in the lesson.

Praise can be a way to scaffold children's language use and understanding. It is not only important to show them how to improve on what they are able to do with language, but also to explain to them what they are doing well, so that they can continue doing this. Praise should always be **formative**, so it is clear to the child *what* they are being praised for and are doing well at. It may use language or can sometimes gestures.

Non-linguistic support might be given to help children understand or communicate. This might include the use of gestures, body language and other actions, for example using **facial expression**, making sounds, nodding and so on.

Teachers may use spoken or written language to scaffold in these ways. Written **feedback** on children's work is particularly relevant for children who are in the upper age range or who have a higher level of reading and writing ability. This may be feedback on an **at-home task**, on a written or oral classroom activity or it could be in written communication with learners or their caregivers, such as an end-of-term report, comments on a class website or blog, and so on. Teacher language is also important when giving clear instructions (orally or as **rubrics** in materials), then checking both the instructions and the children's understanding of concepts or language.

Finally, we should bear in mind that the scaffold may be different for individual children, as we saw earlier with the various types of scaffolding used in construction. It may be used to support and help children at different levels, so that each child can progress in their language learning. We may use language to push children by asking more linguistically challenging questions or making our language slightly more complex when interacting with some children in the class. This will help us *differentiate* our teaching so that we meet the needs of individual children in the class.

Teaching strategies
This is action which the teacher takes, or something the teacher does in order to help children in their understanding and use of language.

Look at some examples of such strategies the teacher could use:

Contextualising language	Here the teacher may use or create a clear and familiar context for language in an activity or text so that children can understand how and when to use language, that is, to give it a clear, logical and genuine purpose. They will understand language better if the context is familiar, and personalising language and activities can also be very valuable for this reason. When children are familiar with the language in a known context or content, then we can move to the less familiar or unknown.
Preparing for an activity	The teacher should provide models of the language the children will need to do an activity, so that it is clear to them what and how to use language. These *models* could be full, or they may simply be prompts to remind children of the language as they do an activity. They could use *props* for this, such as puppets, class mascots or cartoons. This is often combined with demonstration of an activity, which shows the children what to do, so it doesn't rely on their listening skills but provides visual support. Children can also be involved in demonstrations of language and activity. Some key language or content could be *pre-taught* to allow the teacher to focus on skills.
Using the senses	The visual mode is often utilised by teachers to scaffold understanding and language use, and this may be through focusing attention on something visible, such as *realia*, *flashcards*, gestures or movement through *TPR* (Total Physical Response), for example. This may be to support understanding or to help children when they use language to communicate. Children are often more in tune with all their senses than adults in a learning situation, and the senses of smell and taste can also be powerful tools to support understanding and help recall when using language. *Visualisation* – listen and imagine visually in your mind - can be equally valuable in this way (see Unit 9). The sense of touch can be stimulated through the use of realia and textured props.

Language support material	In addition, we can provide extra material to support children as they take part in an activity, or children could make some of these themselves. Examples include **word banks**, picture dictionaries, conversation frames (to supply question/answer stems and structures to build on), prompts and sentence starters, information in the form of charts or tables, and so on. They could be illustrated in different ways to make them more child-friendly, such as using speech bubbles, cartoons or animations.
Managing interaction	Groupwork can be challenging for many children, as they usually have less developed social and interaction skills (e.g. turn-taking). We can use strategies to support learners as they attempt to participate in groupwork, such as: contribution cards or tokens which children 'use up' as they participate; setting a minimum and maximum target (e.g. *'Say at least three words'*); or appointing group managers to encourage or support their peers' interaction. This helps ensure that all children have the opportunity to participate and practise using language. We will look again in more detail at this in Unit 10.

Strategies for challenging fast finishers

As much as every child is unique, every group of children is also unique, and different degrees of scaffolding are needed for each individual and each group. Some may need a lot of support to achieve the learning outcomes, while others may reach them easily. It is important that we challenge all these children and push them to their potential for learning. We often identify these children easily, as they may regularly finish activities before their classmates – without the quality of their work being impacted. We call these children **fast finishers.** It is important to plan for fast finishers in our lessons, and that planning should involve something constructive to do while they wait for others to finish, so that they do not disturb the other children who are still working on the task and are able to push a little further into their potential. It is perhaps tempting to reward children for finishing quickly and letting them play or do something 'fun'; but this is sending out the message that it is speed and completion which are important. In fact, we should encourage children to take care over their work, however easy or difficult they find it – we should focus on *what* they do, not how fast they do it.

Given this, there are a number of ways we can extend learning for fast finishers. An initial step should be to encourage them to check their own work carefully, and this can be encouraged from a young age. Then they could offer help to their partner or others in the group or class, for example by answering their questions, checking their work, explaining something in L1. This may be more suitable for slightly older children who are better able to help rather than to take control and do the work for their partner. Children of any age can be given an *extension activity*. This should be related to the activity or topic, and could extend the vocabulary, provide extra practice or practice using a different skill. For example, they could illustrate and annotate something they have written about or write about something they have talked about with a partner. They could add more words to a word list, create a class dictionary entry or design a review activity for the class. Fast finishers could also review a previous lesson. It is a good idea to develop a bank of generic activities for fast finishers, which can be adapted easily to fit different topics and language.

Depending on the classroom context, children could be given the opportunity to use classroom resources, if the teacher thinks they can do this quietly. They may, for example, choose a **storybook** or *graded reader* from the bookshelf; younger children could be allowed to engage in **free play** with resources used in the English lessons, such as flashcard sets, toy animals, games and so on. This kind of fast finisher activity requires minimal extra planning.

Exploring the concepts in practice

FOLLOW-UP ACTIVITY *(see pages 151–153 for answers)*

 Look at the examples of a teacher scaffolding using language and strategies. Answer the questions.

1 A teacher is setting up an activity with a group of 10–12 lower primary children. They are all sitting in a circle on a carpet on the floor. In the transcript below, we can see the language and strategies this teacher uses to support understanding and use of language.

Read the extract and decide which of the following ways the teacher uses scaffolding:

Teacher language:
1 The teacher grades their language.
2 The teacher repeats or rephrases their language.
3 The teacher asks questions to check children's understanding.
4 The teacher uses or has children use a language other than English.
5 The teacher corrects children's language in different ways.
6 The teacher uses non-linguistic support.
7 The teacher praises the children.

Teaching strategies:
8 Contextualising language
9 Preparing children for an activity
10 Stimulating the senses
11 Providing language support material
12 Managing interaction

Key:

// = overlapping speech
Speech indicated using italics.
The teacher uses exaggerated intonation and sentence stress.
[Actions indicated using square brackets.]

1	Teacher	*One-two-three, eyes on me!* [The teacher uses mime to accompany routine.]
2	Students	*One, two, eyes on you!* [Students mime to accompany routine.]
3	Teacher	*Great. Let's start.* [The teacher takes a card from the pile, looks at it and holds it to their chest so students can't see it.]
		Hmm… What is it? [The teacher stands up and mimes an elephant.]
		It's big and it's grey. What is it?
4	Students	*Elephant.*
5	Teacher	*Is it an elephant? Let's look.* [The teacher turns over the card and shows the students.]
6	Students	*Elephant!*
7	Teacher	*That's right. It's an elephant! Well done!* [The teacher gestures to the students.]
		Who wants to play? Jun? [Jun shakes his head.]
		Kaya? [Kaya nods.]
		OK. Kaya, take a card. Don't show your card. [The teacher gestures 'keeping card hidden'.]
		[Whispers to Kaya] *What…?*
8	Student	*What…*
9	Teacher	*What is…?*
10	Student	*What is it?*
11	Teacher	*Kaya, stand up. Show us the animal.* [Kaya stands up and mimes.]
		Good. Thanks. Tell us, is it big? Small?
12	Student	*Small.*
13	Teacher	*OK.* [To the class] *What is it? What do you think? What is it?*
14	Students	*Snake. // Mouse. // Cat. // Hippo.*
15	Teacher	[The teacher laughs] *Kaya?*
16	Student	*Mice.*
17	Teacher	*OK. Yes. How many?* [The teacher gestures 'one'.]
18	Student	*One.*
19	Teacher	*Yes, one. So, we say one…* [The teacher gestures 'one' and indicates the card.]
20	Students	*Mouse.*
21	Teacher	*That's right. One mouse* [The teacher gestures numbers using fingers.] *and two, three, four, lots of…*
22	Students	*Mice.*
23	Teacher	*Great. So, this is a m…* [The teacher points to card.]
24	Students	*Mouse.*
25	Teacher	*Yes. Thank you, Kaya, you're a super mouse! Who wants a turn?* [The teacher pauses.] *Who wants to play?* [The teacher gestures.]
26		[The teacher repeats model with two more volunteers.]

27 Teacher   *Very good. You're going to play in groups. Jun, number 1. Aiko, number 2. Yoshitaka, number 3, and Mayumi, number 4.* [The teacher gestures.]. *Please play together.* [The teacher has students move so they are sitting in a small circle together. The teacher continues to group students.] *Here are your cards. Please place them face down.* [The teacher distributes cards and indicates face down.] *Remember, do you show the cards?* [The teacher gestures 'show'.] *Or hide the cards? Like a secret?* [The teacher gestures 'hide'.]

28 Students   *Secret. // Hide. //* [Students copy the teacher's gesture for 'hide'.]

29 Teacher   *Yes. And we ask: What…?*

30 Students   *What is it?*

31 Teacher   *Excellent! Who is number one? Raise your hand.* [Number 1 students raise their hands.] *Good. Number 1s, you start. Take a card. Then number 2s. Raise your hand number 2s.* [Number 2s raise their hands.] *OK, you're second…* [The teacher repeats for all numbers.] *Are you ready?*

32 Students   *Yes!*

33 Teacher   *OK. Go!*

2. Look at these examples of teacher language in different situations. How could the teacher improve their language so that they can scaffold the children's understanding or use of language more successfully? Note some improvements the teachers could make.

A Teacher is giving instructions to a class of 11–12-year-olds.
'OK, so, you've got some words, right? Look through them, look through the list on your handout. See if you can find fruit words. Do you understand? OK. Go on, start.'

B Teacher is giving feedback on an activity to a class of 6–7-year-olds.
'Good job, guys! You're amazing!'

C Teacher is explaining a new word to a 6-year-old student.
'You know, it's a kind of tool which people use to cut things. Or chop them up. (…) Food. It's for cutting ingredients. It begins with the letter k.'

D Teacher is checking understanding and drilling a new structure to a class of 9–10-year-olds.

Teacher: *Yes, Mingze?* [shows a flashcard of a girl reading a book]
Mingze: *She… er… reading book.*
Teacher: *No. Try again.*
Mingze: *She reading book?*
Teacher: *She is reading a book. (…) Next. Yan?* [shows a flashcard of a boy riding a bike]
Yan: *He read bike.*
Teacher: *He's riding a bike. Well done.*

Read what the teachers say. To what extent do you agree or disagree with them?

" **Teacher 1:** I speak the same language as the children, so the best way to explain new vocabulary clearly is to give them the translation. "

" **Teacher 2:** I teach mixed level classes, so I often provide support material such as conversation frames with prompts and give plenty of examples. This supports children's language use while letting them choose the language to use in the activity. They can be as creative as they like, or they can use the examples they heard. "

" **Teacher 3:** I try to use a wide variety of props to support children's understanding, including realia, my own photos and photos they bring from home. I find this really useful to provide familiar, relevant contexts and it gives me the opportunity to personalise learning. "

DISCOVERY ACTIVITY

 Choose one or both discovery activities. Follow the steps given.

1. Scaffolding using teacher language
- Audio or video record a part of a lesson you teach.
- Review the recording and transcribe what you say. Analyse your language. What examples of scaffolding can you find in your use of language? Did you miss any opportunities to scaffold using language?
- Identify and try out a kind of scaffolding you haven't used. Think about which part of your next lesson you could you try it in and how you will modify it for different learners in your class, if appropriate. Reflect on how successful it was for your learners' understanding or use of language in the lesson.
- You should check your school policies on data collection and protection before doing this task.

2. Scaffolding using teaching strategies

- Talk to some of the teachers in your school or teaching institution. How many of the senses do they employ in scaffolding strategies?
- Gather their ideas and categorise them into the five senses in a chart. It is likely that they will use mainly sight and sound. Together, brainstorm and add examples for other senses.
- Finally, share your chart with teachers in your school. You could put it on the noticeboard in the teachers' room or share it in editable digital format, for example using Google Documents. Don't forget to leave space for teachers to add more ideas as they have them.

You can use your TKT: YL PD Journal to record and keep track of this investigation. Remember to follow any ethical procedures required by your institution and to ensure you have informed consent of your learners and other participants before collecting any classroom data.

■ TKT: YL Practice task

 Do the practice task for this unit. Try to answer the questions in under ten minutes.
Then check your answers in the answer key on page 158.

For questions **1–6**, match each example to a scaffolding strategy from **A–H**. There are two extra options which you don't need.

Scaffolding strategies

A Allowing wait time after asking a question
B Moving from known to unknown in an activity
C Using visual aids to support meaning
D Revising language children need for a task
E Demonstrating an activity through a model
F Using the children's L1 when appropriate
G Relating activities to children's experience
H Creating opportunities for learning through one of the five senses (smell or taste)

1

Teacher: *Everybody, please close your eyes. Now, I'm going to pass you something on a plate. Tell me, what is it? Don't open your eyes, don't taste it and don't touch it! What is it? OK, here we go. Jassim?*
Jassim: *Oh! Er... chocolate.*
Teacher: *Yes! That's right. How do you know?*
Jassim: *I use nose.*

2 A teacher writes in their *lesson plan*:

Stage 1	Pre-teaching	Show animal flashcards. Say the words and have children mime the animals. Show the flashcards again and have children repeat the words as they mime.
Stage 2	Listening activity	Hand out flashcards. Play the farm animal song. Children...

3 Part of teacher instructions for a pairwork task:

Teacher: *María Teresa, you're going to ask the question. First, who can remind María Teresa of the question?*

José: *What time do you.. er.. get up?*

Teacher: *That's right, José, well done. Let's all practise together: What time do you get up? Everyone: What time do you get up?*

4 Teacher's introduction to an activity:

Teacher: *Have you ever got lost somewhere? What did you do? Yes, Louline? Tell us about it...*

Louline: *I, with my family, went to shopping. I lose my mother in the shop.*

Teacher: How did you feel? What did you do?
[Teacher exchanges with Louline about her experience.]

Teacher: *So, we're going to do some drama. You are with your family at the museum, but you lost them somewhere in the museum....*

5

Teacher: *The main character in the story is Ben, isn't it? What is Ben like, do you think?*
[Teacher looks slowly around the class. There is no response. Teacher pauses a few seconds longer.]

Teacher: *Ndeye, what do you think? Tell me about Ben. What is he like?*

6

Kazu: *Ge-mu ga suki. I.. er.. I like... nan da? Ge-mu. I like ge-mu.*

Teacher: *Ah, you like video games? Ge-mu in English is video games.*

Unit 9 Classroom activities for language practice: How can I use practice activities to consolidate children's language learning?

LEARNING OUTCOMES

By the end of this unit, you will…
KNOWLEDGE: know about the importance of practice activities in language learning
SKILLS: be able to identify demands and appropriate support for learners when using different language practice activities

■ Starter Question

Before you begin this unit, read the starter question and make some notes. Then read the commentary and compare it to your notes.

 Why are language practice activities an important element a language lesson? **Note two or three reasons.**

COMMENTARY

What is a practice activity?
Simply put, a **practice activity** is one where learners use the skills and language that are being focused on in the lesson (or series of lessons). This language is often known as **target language** and may be a grammatical structure, vocabulary items, set phrases, **functional language** or **chunks**. The practice may be spoken or written if it is **productive**, or it may involve listening or reading if it is **receptive**; it may focus on **subskills** of these skills.

Why practise?
It seems clear that in order to learn to speak a language, we should use it – consider the expression, *'Practice makes perfect'*. However, in some teaching and learning contexts, language is seen as a subject to study, rather than something we learn to use. In such a situation, learners may practise only rarely and as a result, at the end of their studies they may know a lot about language, but are often less able to use the language in communication with another speaker of that language.

Constructivist learning theories tell us that learners need to be *active* in the learning process – they are not passive receivers of knowledge, but actively build their understanding of concepts and language. Meanwhile, behaviourist views say we learn from mimicking and memorising language. Interactionists, on the other hand, suggest we learn through communicating and negotiating meaning with others (see Lightbown & Spada, 2021, especially Chapters 4 and 6, for an in-depth look at second language learning theories). While some of these and other theories are more influential than others in modern thinking, we can clearly see the importance for learners to have the opportunity to actually practise using the language, trying it out and getting used to it. In this way, the language becomes more automatic and easily accessible for communication in real time as it passes from short-term memory to long-term memory (Harmer, 2007, p. 85). This is known as *internalisation*.

In order for internalisation to happen, we should plan for *deliberate practice* activities (Pinter, 2006, p. 85) which engage and actively involve all the learners in the class and which provide plenty of repetition of language in different meaningful situations and contexts, over a period of time.

■ Key concepts

> Reflect on the *key concept* question. Brainstorm your ideas, then expand your notes as you read.
>
> *What are some key features of an effective practice activity?* **Name at least three.**

COMMENTARY

Practice activities can vary widely in their type, their ***goal*** and, of course, their focus. For a practice activity to be successful in its purpose, it should:

- *Have a clear language teaching **objective**(s).*
  The learning objectives of the activity should relate to and specify the target language being taught, which means that the learners will be using the target language in the activity.

- *Have a well-defined language-oriented **outcome**(s).*
  This is what the children will produce or gain from the activity. It could be a written (e.g. a poster, a blog post, a sentence) or spoken (an answer to a question, a dialogue, a single word) product; it may be a process outcome, such as a skill or attitude (e.g. gain in confidence, improved ***collaborative*** skills) or a communicative outcome (e.g. to ask for something in a shop). It is important to keep in mind our learners' needs when considering learning outcomes and objectives.

- *Have a clearly identifiable and meaningful purpose.*
  Learners should see a reason for using the language, ideally a real purpose (e.g. to find out personal information in a survey, to find differences between two pictures, to create a classroom display). The objectives and outcomes, therefore, will shift away from a linguistic focus, for example:

  > To practise 'families' vocabulary. (linguistic objective) becomes: To find out about your friend's family.

This will motivate learners as well as provide a ***context*** for language and language practice.

- *Engage all learners in language practice.*
An activity which requires just one or two learners in the class to use the language does not give everyone the same opportunity to practise. Pair or small group activities are often useful to ensure that all learners get the opportunity to use language, whereas **whole class** teacher-student interactions or **open pairs** give that opportunity only to those who the teacher chooses.

- *Provide repeated opportunity for practice.*
In a practice activity, have students use the target language or skill more than once. For example, they may ask three questions about their partner's family, or talk to two friends in the classroom. Where possible, provide more than one practice activity so that children can meet and use the language in different contexts.

- *Require the use of L2, whose form is clear to learners.*
Where an activity can't be undertaken as easily in English, learners may resort to using their own language (L1) to do the activity, especially in a monolingual class setting. Similarly, learners need to have the linguistic resources (i.e. some knowledge of the right language) to carry out the activity. It may be that it is a specific form to be practised or it may be that they are choosing or using language of their own choice. If this is unclear or unknown to learners, they are again likely to revert to their L1. The **model** of language form(s) is likely to have come from **input** given before the activity begins.

- *Stimulate and motivate learners.*
A practice activity which stimulates learners' thinking and provides the right amount of challenge will motivate them to engage in the activity. If the level of challenge is too high, however, it will make it difficult for them to focus on the language practice itself. A fun activity can be inherently motivating, but if it is too easy or does not engage learners' thinking skills, then that **motivation** may quickly disappear. We will consider this point in more detail in the next section.

Controlled and free practice

In **controlled practice**, the language and context are pre-defined and the learners are repeating language they have heard (or read). This could be spoken or written; in the case of controlled practice, the response is fixed, and the focus is inherently on **form** (the structure of the target language). It is important, however, that there is also a **focus on meaning** in controlled practice. These kinds of activity give an important opportunity for learners to hear new language and practise articulating it in context, so are useful when focusing on pronunciation in particular, and also contribute to internalisation of new language. They are usually **accuracy**-focused.

Free practice activities, on the opposite end of the scale, are those where learners can use whatever language they wish to complete a task. These kinds of task and activity may focus on developing **fluency** and encourage learners to put together different language they have learned in order to interact to do the activity. There is often greater scope for **personalisation** with free activities.

Most activities will come somewhere between tightly controlled and completely free, so may be described as 'more/less controlled' or 'freer/less free'. It is possible to place activity types on a cline, although the degree of language support the teacher gives will have an effect on the degree of control/freedom.

More controlled

Drills are when learners listen to a model, often the teacher but it may be from an audio or video clip, and repeat what they hear. They often involve simple repetition, or the teacher might ask learners to change words, in response to some kind of input, such as a flashcard or word card. This is known as a *substitution drill*.

Gap-fills, sentence completion, reordering and other activities where learners manipulate language or answer *closed questions* are often controlled activities because there is a single, fixed answer. They can be written or spoken and can utilise visuals or movement to help stimulate and motivate young learners.

Games, puzzles and quizzes often require a fixed response, so are also a form of controlled practice. Wordsearches, crosswords and other word **games** are useful for focusing on form (e.g. spelling), while a wide range of games and game-like activities might require learners to use fixed phrases, expressions or vocabulary when playing, so can also sometimes be classed as controlled.

Surveys and questionnaires may be more or less free depending on the degree of freedom learners have when creating the questions as well as the kinds of responses they require from the respondents.

Information gap activities often require learners to use specific question forms and/or responses. Generally speaking, the information itself is controlled, so the teacher can predict vocabulary and target language.

Role plays and other **drama** activities could be placed higher or lower on the cline, depending on the extent to which learners write their own scripts and are supported in doing so.

Problem-solving, researching, sharing ideas and experiences, sequencing and similar activity types are likely to be freer activities, although a *language frame* could be used to support learners, adding a degree of control.

Discussions and debates may require learners to draw on all their language resources, which can be difficult for the teacher to predict. However, a teacher could provide support by supplying functional language, such as phrases for making or refuting an argument.

Free play gives younger learners the opportunity to practise language they have learned. Although they may choose to practise specific target language, perhaps by singing a song or repeating a dialogue from class in play, the choice to do this is the child's, so this can be classified as freer.

Freer

Finally, it is important to note that when designing any practice activity, however controlled or free, it is essential that there is a clear, meaningful, age-appropriate context. Wherever possible, there should be the possibility for personalisation, which makes practice relevant and relatable to the learner.

Key concepts and the YL classroom

Reflect on the *key concepts and the YL classroom* question. Brainstorm your ideas, then expand your notes as you read.

 What considerations do or should you make when planning a practice activity for young learners especially? **Identify two or three considerations.**

COMMENTARY

In Part 1 of this book, we looked at developing learning, cognitive and communication strategies through language learning, and saw examples of activities which might allow us to develop these areas. In the language classroom, these activities will naturally be geared towards language learning through practice. We can see, then, that similar principles apply for practice activities, most notably that we should use activities which support the child in different areas of development alongside language; we should focus on **whole-child development.**

When considering practice activity selection or design for young learners, it is particularly important to think about what the learner actually needs to do in order to succeed at an activity. A simple, controlled drill, for example, may require learners to listen, articulate and repeat something in English: there is minimal cognition involved in this activity; it will be relatively easy for learners to achieve and, therefore, to have practice of the target language. On the other hand, a more complicated activity, such as a game with a sequence of steps or rules, or a collaborative problem-solving activity might require the use of social skills and *HOTS (Higher Order Thinking Skills),* so learners need to think carefully about what they are doing as well as the language they are using. Cameron (2001) identifies six types of task demand. The degree of need to account for these demands will vary according to the child's age as well as other individual factors, such as their social-emotional skills, **motor skills**, *attention span* and so on. Cameron's (2001, p. 25) task demands include:

- *Cognitive demands*: Interpreting the activity input and procedures (e.g. a need to read a clock; understanding what is shown in illustrations).
- *Language demands:* Whether it is oral or written, the grammar form needed; the degree of requirement for use of L2.
- *Interactional demands:* Whether it requires collaboration or co-operation, such as in pair work, group work, interacting with a teacher, etc.
- *Metalinguistic demands:* The use of technical language in instructions, talking about language, etc.

- *Involvement demands*: How easily the child is engaged and stays engaged: linked to interest, length of steps, etc.
- *Physical demands*: The amount of movement and sitting still; the need for fine motor skills.

When planning practice activities, we should consider all kinds of demand so that we can understand how best to support children in accomplishing the activity and practising the language: in other words, so that they can reach the learning objectives and outcomes of the lesson. Look at some practice activity examples:

Stirrers and settlers

The principle of stirrers and settlers is that we manage children's natural energy and excitement levels using a pattern of active (usually physically and involving groups or whole class), exciting activities where children can expend energy (*stirrer*, such as a ***TPR (Total Physical Response)*** game), followed by a quiet, calm, often individual activity, sitting at tables (*settler*, such as a ***coursebook***, workbook or art activity). In turn, this should be followed by another stirrer, then a settler, and so on. In this way, we can manage children's physical and interactional needs to help them focus individually for an activity with higher cognitive and/or language demands.

Competitive and co-operative activities

Many children love competing with others, and this can motivate them to participate in an activity. However, competition does not favour all children and can take away from our efforts to help children develop a love for learning and for English – their motivation becomes instrumental rather than intrinsic.

Co-operative activities which require all children to participate and take on a role in an activity often involve group work. Children may have a specific role in the group or may have specific information in a ***jigsaw*** or information gap activity. These kinds of activity have high interactional demand and will help children develop social-emotional skills. Some children may need the teacher's support to interact with their peers; care is needed when deciding how to group children so that they are able to co-operate well.

It is therefore important to favour co-operative activities, although an occasional competitive game can be fun as a warmer or cooler.

Songs, chants, rhymes and poems

There are many examples of these kinds of activity, and nowadays, source material is often easily available online. Depending how we use these, they may provide very controlled practice (e.g. by singing a song or repeating a chant which utilises specific language, exactly how it is heard, such as a *Hello!* song), or it could be freer if we encourage learners to create new verses or lines or to respond to them as input. They might describe a character, scene or item in a poem, or draw and talk about something in a ***rhyme*** using adjectives of their choice, for example. These kinds of activity not only cater to children's interest in music and rhythm, but can also be combined with TPR, dancing or drama, and are naturally appealing and familiar to children. They are ideal for focusing on pronunciation and rhythm, i.e. word and sentence stress. Children may become excited when they are active, so may need reminding of the target language being practised.

Cognitive activities

These include activities such as: memory activities (e.g. flashcard games such as **pelmanism**, quizzes); categorisation, ranking, sequencing or ordering activities (e.g. grouping food words based on characteristics or preference); problem-solving activities (e.g. **webquests**, mystery adventure or detective games, escape room games). The degree of control of language will vary depending on the activity, but the cognitive demands of these activities is often high. If children struggle with such activities, they may need task support to be able to practise the target language; their difficulties may not be caused by a lack of understanding of the language.

Stories

Storybooks can be a rich source of highly contextualised language and can be used in different ways. The teacher may read to the children and focus on particular language in activities before, while and after reading. Older children may read short stories such as *graded readers*. The language demands may be high as children will probably encounter a lot of new language. It is important, therefore, for the children to learn to focus on key information and language to understand particular aspects of the story, rather than to attempt to understand every detail or word. Similarly, the teacher may tell stories to the children, using mime, *gestures*, voice and perhaps visuals to support their understanding of specific language and the story as a whole.

Listen (or read) and respond

We may have learners listen to something and show their understanding by responding in some way, for example: listen-and-do, listen-and-make, listen-and-draw, listen-and-say, listen-and-visualise or -imagine, listen-and-write, listen-and-act. *Dictation* is an example of this kind of activity, e.g. *picture dictation*. The response activity could be more or less controlled depending how it is structured, although the teacher usually has control over the language input in the listening stage. Note that the input could be given by a student (e.g. in a pair or group activity), or be a written text, at sentence or paragraph level for older children, or at word level for children who have less developed *literacy* skills. We should consider the demands of both the listening aspect of the activity and the response, and offer support accordingly, perhaps by repeating what is said, pausing, giving models of the response.

■ Exploring the concepts in practice

FOLLOW-UP ACTIVITY *(see pages 153–155 for answers)*

 Look at the extracts from published materials showing practice activities, and answer the questions.

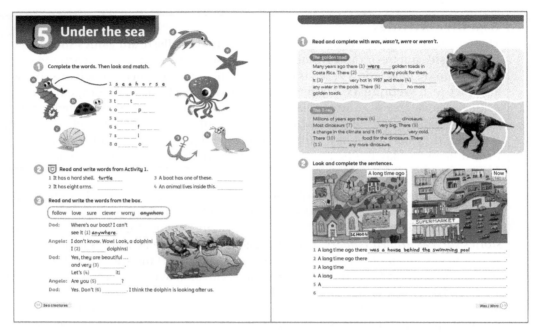

Extract 1: Puchta, Lewis-Jones, Gerngross and Zagouras (2022) *Super Minds Level 3* 2nd Edition Workbook, pp. 26–27: Cambridge University Press & Assessment

1 What kinds of activity are these? Which, if any, is/are an example of:
   - Matching
   - Short answer question
   - MCQ (multiple choice question)
   - Visualisation
   - Gap-fill
   - Crossword puzzle
   - Sentence completion
2 What exactly are learners practising in each activity?
3 How might you categorise the five activities as: controlled; less controlled; freer; free?
4 What demands on learners are important to consider for each activity?
5 What kind of support is given to learners in each activity?

17 What's on the menu?

Do the food project!

o Learners look for information about food they are not familiar with. They can then make a poster.

o They can include information on where the food comes from, if it grows on a tree, in the ground, etc.

o For example: *(Pineapples) are fruit. They're (yellow, brown and green.) They grow (on plants) in hot countries, for example, (Australia, Costa Rica). People eat pineapples for (breakfast/ lunch/dinner).*

o You can display the posters around the classroom.

Suggested sources

http://www.foodafactoflife.org.uk/sheet.aspx?siteId=15&sectionId= 64&contentId=49

http://www.sciencekids.co.nz/sciencefacts/food.html

15

PHOTOCOPIABLE © Cambridge University Press 2015

Look at Extract 2. Are these statements True or False?

1 This is a very controlled practice activity.

2 This activity practises past simple for describing condition, state and habits.

3 The teacher could support learners by providing a sentence frame such as in the third point shown. This would make the activity more controlled.

4 Learners practise mostly Speaking and Listening in this activity.

5 Learners could work collaboratively in a group in this activity.

Extract 2: Robinson and Saxby (2015) *Cambridge English Fun for Starters Additional Resources for Teachers,* p. 15: Cambridge University Press & Assessment

REFLECTION

 Look in a coursebook or other learning materials you use in your classes, or have access to. Find two or more example practice activities. Copy the table below into your notes and complete it.

Activity reference (Source + page number/link):	*Activity type:*	*Category* (controlled-free):	*Practice in* (target language or skills):
Activity description (including objectives and outcomes):			

Activity demands:	Support:

To what extent does it:
- Have a clear and meaningful purpose?
- Engage all learners in practice?
- Provide repeated opportunity for practice?
- Require the use of L2?
- Stimulate and motivate learners?

How might you improve this practice activity for your learners?

DISCOVERY ACTIVITY

 Try the discovery activity to explore teaching and learning in your context.

A: Identify a practice activity type from this unit that is new to you.
B: Plan to use it in your teaching:
- Write a language practice objective for this activity.
- Think about the demands and support you should give your learners.
- Plan the activity as part of a complete lesson.

C: Teach the lesson and observe the learners practising the language.
D: Reflect.
- How effective was the activity in meeting the language practice objectives?
- Did learners have the right amount/type of support relative to the demands of the activity?

If you do not currently teach young learners, you could ask another teacher if you can work with them or their class. Alternatively, you could either do steps A and B only OR Steps C and D using a recording of a lesson you've found online.

You can use your TKT: YL PD Journal to record and keep track of your work. Remember to follow any ethical procedures required by your institution and to ensure you have informed consent of your learners and other participants before collecting any classroom data.

■ TKT: YL Practice task

 Do the practice task for this unit. Try to answer the questions in under ten minutes.

Then check your answers in the answer key on page 158.

For questions **1–6**, look at the description of teaching and/or learning. Then read the related statements **A–C**. Which ONE statement (**A–C**) is **NOT** true?

1   Learners sit in a circle and sing a *'How are you?'* song at the beginning of each lesson. The teacher then asks some children *'How are you today?'*; the children reply using different adjectives, based on how they are really feeling: *'I'm…. How about you?'*

   A   Learners are practising pronunciation in a controlled way when singing the song.
   B   The song uses TPR.
   C   The teacher-learner interaction is freer than the singing activity.

2   Learners play a team game where they write as many words as possible within three minutes into a chart on the topic of *transport*.

   A   This is a brainstorming activity.
   B   Learners are practising writing at sentence level.
   C   The teacher could support interactional demands by setting a limit to the number of words each learner in the group can contribute.

3   Pairs of learners complete a drawing of a make-believe animal by adding different body parts, coloured patterns and giving their animal superpowers, using a template. In new pairs, learners dictate their picture to their new partner, who completes a new template. Learners return to their original partners. They now have three animal pictures. They make sentences to compare the animals using adjectives in the superlative form.

   A   The stages in this activity move from controlled practice to free practice.
   B   Learners can be creative with language in the initial stage of the activity.
   C   Learners practise speaking and listening with more than one partner.

4   The teacher would like learners to practise speaking using food vocabulary they have been working on in the lesson.

   A   Learners could do an information-gap activity in pairs, where they each have similar pictures of a market stall and should find the differences between them.
   B   Learners could do a memory activity, where they look at pictures of plates of food for one minute, then tell their partner what was on each plate.
   C   Learners could do a visualisation activity, where they listen to a recording then draw a picture.

5   A teacher would like to plan practice activities which involve a high cognitive demand.

   A   The teacher could choose a problem-solving activity.
   B   The teacher could choose a ***choral drill***.
   C   The teacher could choose a memory activity.

6 The teacher works with a school in a different country to set up an e-pal project.
Learners in the two schools meet each other online through video call and then
communicate with each other by email, at first as a whole class and then individually.
The project lasts for the whole school year.

   A This activity allows free language practice.

   B Learners may be motivated by a genuine context and need for English language
   use to communicate.

   C Learners are likely to need minimal support for this activity.

Unit 10   Managing learning: How can I manage children in class?

■ Starter Question

Before you begin this unit, read the starter question and make some notes. Then read the commentary and compare it to your notes.

 What does the term 'classroom management' mean to you?

COMMENTARY

'Classroom management' is an extremely broad area and covers all teacher skills and strategies which are done in the classroom to ensure as much learning happens as is possible. It is a practical classroom-based aspect of teaching and one which can give rise to many a teacher concern, when not handled appropriately. The *TKT Glossary* defines ***classroom management*** as follows:

> 'The things teachers do to organise the classroom, the learning and the learners, such as organising seating arrangements, organising different types of activities and managing interaction patterns' (p. 7).

Most teachers aim for a classroom where their learners are engaged and productive, and where they feel secure and confident to make every effort to learn. In such a positive learning environment, learners will achieve to the best of their ability and the teacher will also be positive and motivated. However, the well-developed organisational skills and confidence the teacher needs to achieve this can take time and effort to acquire.

■ Key concepts

Reflect on the key concept question. Brainstorm your ideas, then expand your notes as you read.

 How can teachers develop a positive classroom atmosphere to promote learning? Note up to three points.

COMMENTARY

As we can infer from the definition on the previous page, there are several areas of classroom management teachers need to be aware of and develop in order to create a classroom where learners are motivated, respected, confident and willing to learn. We can break these down into six main areas:
1. Organising the classroom
2. Organising the learners
3. Organising learning
4. Managing time
5. Developing a respectful relationship with learners
6. Interacting with learners

1. Organising the classroom

How can I best organise my classroom?

- How to make effective use of classroom space
- How to arrange the furniture
- How to organise materials and resources

Classrooms vary greatly in their physical layout, and institutions vary in the degree of freedom they give teachers to modify this. Creating a welcoming, comfortable and English **print-rich** classroom is an initial step towards developing a positive learning atmosphere where all learners feel secure and ready to learn.

The board and screen, if available, should be easily and comfortably visible to all learners. Some classrooms have different areas, spaces and resources, especially those for younger learners in the age range. These might include:
- a large carpet for **circle time**, story time and other *whole-class* activities.
- a play, reading or relaxation area, where resources such as storybooks, *graded readers*, *props*, visuals and other materials used in class can be kept so they are available for learners to use freely.
- visible and accessible display areas and noticeboards, where the class can create spaces for temporary and semi-permanent, interactive and static displays of learners' work.

Tables are usually best arranged so that students can sit in groups. This will help them work together, share ideas and resources, and *collaborate* on activities such as *projects* or art and craft. It will also give more space in the classroom to move around for both the teacher and the students. In some teaching contexts, it may not be possible to move tables and chairs, or they may need to be left at the end of the lesson as they were found at the beginning. Build in routines where the children help to organise the furniture, or get up to move to each other's tables for pair or group activities. Learners will quickly become accustomed to these routines and be able to do them quickly.

A print-rich environment is one where written text of different forms can be seen in the classroom: this may be displays, but also includes notices, posters (e.g. with useful language or classroom behaviour expectations or rules, which can be clearly pointed towards when necessary), labelling of furniture, resources and so on. Much of the text is added gradually during the term or year and may include learners' work. This constantly visible text will gradually become familiar and well-known to all learners who use the classroom.

2. Organising the learners

- How to pair and group learners
- How to arrange seating

There are different ways we might pair or group learners, depending on an activity, on the learners and on the learning *context*. *Pairs* could, for example, mix or put together learners based on language level, gender, age, personality and other individual factors.

While younger learners may be accepting of an assigned partner or group member, they may have less developed interactional or social skills, so may find it challenging to work with other children. Older learners, especially from around 10 or 11 years old, may have stronger preferences as to who they work with. The teacher may also have their own reasons for pairing or grouping in the way they do.

It is common for teachers to pair and group based on level, where a stronger learner may support a weaker one. While this is often effective, it is equally true that stronger learners together will push each other's learning, and lower level learners can support each other at their level. Often, *mixed level* pairings are effective for *controlled* activities, while same level pairings work well for *freer* activities. Similarly, while grouping friends together can make the learning experience more enjoyable, it may be more difficult to manage behaviour. It is important to consider individual preferences, although it is equally important for young learners to learn to work with different people. As such, varying pairs and groups is key; also, sometimes using a technique to assign learners randomly.

The classroom should be set up in such a way that pair and groupwork is facilitated by the position of the tables or desks. Where furniture is fixed, learners could move their chairs or stand around one table or even in a small circle away from the tables. The classroom layout should never prevent interaction in the classroom.

3. Organising learning

- How to organise activities
- How to manage interaction
- How to encourage learners to be responsible for their own learning

We saw in Unit 9 that alternating *stirrers* and *settlers* can help manage learners' energy levels to allow them to focus on learning. We have also seen that *routines* can help learners understand and develop responsible behaviour and feel secure in the classroom through their familiarity.

There are different *interaction patterns* available for teachers to employ in the classroom, as we have seen (pair work, group work, individual work, for example). We have seen ways in which we can group and pair learners, and it is equally important to think about how we set up interactions and how we interact with learners, such as when the teacher addresses or asks a question to the whole class. We might insist that children raise their hands to answer a question or *elicit* information, which can help keep control of a class, while *nominating* learners directly allows us to check progress and understanding for specific children. Care is needed to ensure that all children are given the opportunity to contribute and participate without fear or embarrassment. Nominating should never be used as a punishment, to shame or to test an individual in front of the class.

Finally, we can encourage children to gradually take control of their own learning and foster a sense of belonging by giving them responsibilities in the classroom and encouraging them to manage their own learning and behaviour. This may be done by having class monitors, whose responsibilities might include keeping resources and displays tidy, cleaning the board, overseeing the use of English in the classroom, and so on. Having a responsibility in the classroom builds children's self-esteem and sense of belonging and allows them to become more independent learners. This can be further strengthened by encouraging learners to take care of and organise their work, to set and review learning *goals* and plan their work.

4. Managing time

- How to plan lesson time
- How to use time limits and countdowns
- How to manage transitions

> **How can I best manage time?**

Lesson plans should always consider the timing of different stages in a lesson, taking into account the time needed for setting up and feeding back after activities as well as the time needed for the activity itself. We noted in Unit 8 that fast finishers should also be planned for, and some teachers plan an if-time flexi-stage, which they decide to use or not as the lesson progresses. This also allows adequate time for the later stages of the lesson, which are quite often the ones where learners are working on the most meaningful and motivating activities.

In the classroom itself, the first key step is to tell learners how long they have for an activity. After that time has elapsed, stop learners. You may give extra time if needed, or you might choose to stop the activity if most learners are finished. Using a timer, writing the finish time on the board or having a countdown are useful. There are plenty of tools available online which can be used with a projector or *interactive whiteboard* and have their own sounds. Being clear – but realistic – about timing helps learners manage the pace of their work and understand time as a concept, especially younger learners.

Transitions are the moments in the classroom where we move from one activity to another. There are various techniques we can use to mark that time, and routines are a valuable strategy to help students stop working, tidy up as necessary and change focus to a new task or to listening to new instructions. Transition routines may include a song or *chant*, or could involve a clear signal from the teacher or action by the children. Clear transitions help children organise themselves and re-focus their thinking quickly onto a new learning activity. Over a year, they are a valuable opportunity for extra learning, like any routine.

5. Developing a respectful relationship with learners

- – How to develop a positive teacher personality
- – How to use your voice
- – How to interact with learners
- – How to get and keep learners' attention

Teacher presence is the ability to respectfully 'own' the class, to show and be in control by gaining and holding the attention of the class when necessary. A strong teacher presence will generally require:

- an assertive – but not aggressive – personality, which learners feel confident in but not afraid of.
- a strong, clear voice which projects well but doesn't shout angrily.
- a preference for positive reinforcement of good behaviour to negative reactions to challenging behaviour, such as punishment.
- a mobile teacher, who frequently moves around the classroom to instruct, *monitor* learning, speak privately to individuals and give feedback to the whole class.
- an accessible teacher, who learners feel uninhibited to speak to (physically or emotionally).
- a teacher who uses appropriate strategies to get learners' attention and to maintain it, never instructing or beginning an activity unless all learners know what is expected of them.

6. Interacting with learners

- – How to respond to learners' individual needs
- – How to use Teacher Talking Time
- – How to correct effectively

Teacher presence is also impacted by the way in which we interact with our learners. To gain their respect, it is important to view and treat them as individuals, to make an effort to get to know each learner and to be sensitive to their needs in our classroom management and lesson planning. Initially, learning and using their names will help foster the relationship, but we can also find out about learners' personality traits, interests and preferences to help fine-tune the learning outcomes of our lessons and materials.

We interact with our learners using language, and in many contexts the teacher is the main source of exposure to English. We should try to use English as much as possible in our class, although may reserve the learners' first language for dealing with specific problems or for supporting learners' emotional needs. *Teacher Talking Time (TTT)* is the amount of class time we spend speaking English to learners. While quality TTT is valuable input, we also should try to maximise *STT (student talking time*, that is when all students are using English) in order to ensure plenty of opportunity for language practice to all learners. All teacher talk should be clear, concise and *graded* to the learners' level, and supported through *gestures*, demonstration, visuals and so on, as needed. It is rarely essential to instruct in L1, and in cases where this occurs frequently, learners will miss out on the opportunity for input from the teacher.

In *accuracy*-focused, controlled practice activities, mistakes in *target language* may need correction by the teacher, the learner themselves or a peer. This should be done sensitively and in a measured way. Allowing learners to share answers with a partner before whole-class feedback (**Think-Pair-Share**) will encourage *peer correction* and reduce potential stress of speaking in front of the class. When focusing on *fluency*, teachers may make a note of common mistakes in target language and then deal with them (anonymously) in *plenary*, perhaps in form of a quiz or game to correct as a class.

Some other factors that impact on classroom management may be outside the teacher's control. These can depend heavily on context, but might include external factors, such as noise from air-conditioning, construction or a road nearby, the weather, limitations imposed by school rules, cultural, political or religious influences, access to technology and other facilities, such as internet or a library, and so on. It is the teacher's responsibility to make themselves aware of such external influences and try their best to find solutions.

■ Key concepts and the YL classroom

> Reflect on the *key concepts and the YL classroom* question. Brainstorm your ideas, then expand your notes as you read.
>
> *Teachers of young learners sometimes encounter challenging behaviour. What kind of classroom manager might be able to deal with these issues effectively?*

COMMENTARY

Despite our best efforts to develop a positive learning environment and to develop a strong rapport with our learners, teachers of young learners may face challenging learner behaviour in their lessons. By working on our classroom management style from the beginning, we may reduce the likelihood of such problems. We might do this by keeping six Cs in mind:

✓ Be **clear** about your expectations of appropriate behaviour; be clear about what you want the children to do and say in an activity.

✓ Be **consistent** in your response to learners, whether it involves praise or reacting to challenging behaviour. Treat all learners equally and follow through on what you say (do what you say you will).

> **6 Cs of classroom management:**
> Be Clear, Consistent, Calm, Considerate, Communicative and Collaborative.

✓ Be **calm** and avoid anger and shouting when facing a challenging situation. You will be able to think more clearly and the learners will not lose their respect for you.

✓ Be **considerate** towards the learners. A learner may behave poorly when there is a separate, personal issue, and he or she is looking for your attention or sympathy. Meanwhile, consider the other learners in the group and minimise the impact on them.

✓ Be **communicative** by allowing the learner to have their say and express their opinions. If you encounter unexpected bad behaviour, try to find out from the learner what might have caused it. It is important to first find out why this situation has occurred. You may want to use learners' L1 to ensure you are both communicating well, if this is an option.

✓ Be **collaborative** with learners in their learning by negotiating classroom rules, learning content and *objectives* and assessment strategies. This will help them take ownership over their learning and become more independent learners.

Above all, if you frequently encounter challenging behaviour and are trying out a new technique to manage it, don't give up easily – be persistent. Seek help from other teachers in your school or network. It is likely they may have encountered similar problems with the same learner(s), class, or context. And finally, if a situation arises where any child is at risk, you should seek help from another adult. Never leave a classroom with young learners unattended, and never exclude a child from your classroom.

■ Exploring the concepts in practice

FOLLOW-UP ACTIVITY *(see page 155 for answers)*

 Read teachers' classroom management challenges. How would you advise these teachers? Make a note of your answer.
Then match each challenge to a possible solution. To what extent are these the same as your suggestions?

Challenges:

Teacher 1: *A student in my Year 3 class (8 years old) often shouts out silly answers when I ask the whole class questions. I find it very irritating and get quite annoyed with the student. I don't know why she won't stop!*

Teacher 2: *Sometimes when I want to start a new activity, the children just carry on with the previous one. So, I just give instructions to the class anyway, and then go to each student and try to get them to move to the next activity.*

Teacher 3: *Often, I give instructions and tell students to start, but they just sit there and don't do anything! I ask them if they understand what to do, and they say yes. I don't know why they don't get on task quickly.*

Teacher 4: *My 9–10-year-old students sit at desks individually in their own classroom. The teachers must leave the classrooms in the way they found them, so I never move the desks. But it is very difficult to do pair, group and mingling activities.*

Possible solutions:

Solution A: You could use a transitions routine. For example, when it's time to finish an activity, use an online count-down. When time's up, chant '1-2-3, eyes on me!', students stop what they are doing and reply '1-2, eyes on you!'. Then you can tell them to put their materials away, and begin instructing the next activity. Make sure you set clear time limits!

Solution B: It's likely that some or all of the children haven't understood the instructions or weren't paying attention when you gave them. Make sure you always have their full attention before giving instructions. Use plenty of demonstrating and check their understanding by asking *closed questions*, such as 'How many words do you need to write?' or 'Are you working alone or with your partner?'

Solution C: Try to stay calm and avoid showing anger as this could weaken your presence in the classroom. You could try to manage participation by giving learners tokens, which they 'spend' to answer a question; ignore any answers given without raising hands and being invited to answer, and reward the children who do raise their hands.

Solution D: You could ask students to move their desks to make pairs or groups, or the desks could be pushed to the side of the room for mingling activities and other whole-class activities. At the end of the lesson, the children can help put their desks back into position. Alternatively, students could stand to do some activities, or they could gather around one desk, or even go outside to the playground or another communal area.

> **REFLECTION**

 Choose one or more of these reflection activities which will suit your context.

Activity 1
Arrange to meet other teachers in your school, community or professional learning group. Share your classroom management challenges by giving just one or two each. Work together to suggest solutions to these problems. If possible, regroup after a period of time so you can report back to the group on the outcome of these suggested solutions.

Activity 2

Write your own 'Six Classroom Management Top Tips'. Try to focus on different areas of classroom management we have seen in this unit. Share it with other teachers in your school, community or professional learning group to get their *feedback*. Ask them to add to your six tips so that you can develop a longer list, then share the longer list.

Activity 3

At the beginning of the year or course, spend some time with your learners talking about and sharing expectations. In groups or as a whole class, students write a classroom expectations poster. Put this in a prominent place in your classroom so you – and the students – can refer to it when necessary.

DISCOVERY ACTIVITY

 Look at the two discovery activities to explore classroom management in your context. Choose one to do which is most useful in your context.

Activity 1

Plan and write a short survey to find out from your students what they think makes an effective teacher, for example their management style, their use of language and strategies and other areas which are relevant or particular to your context.
Gather and reflect on the data from the survey. Develop two or three action points for your own development. Share the survey findings and your action points with your class. Return to this after a specified time and reflect on any changes.

Activity 2

Record yourself interacting with your students in the classroom (audio or video). Analyse the recording so you focus on the way in which you use your language to manage the class. Reflect on your analysis:
- To what extent did you achieve the 6Cs?
- Which of the 6Cs were your strengths?
- What areas could you improve upon?

Write an action plan, including what you hope to improve on, how you will do it, and over what period of time. After that time, record another lesson and reanalyse your language. What changes do you notice?

You can use your TKT: YL PD Journal to record and keep track of your work. Remember to follow any ethical procedures required by your institution and to ensure you have informed consent of your learners and other participants before collecting any classroom data.

■ TKT: YL Practice task

> ⏱ **Do the practice task for this unit. Try to answer the questions in under ten minutes.**
> **Then check your answers in the answer key on page 158.**

For questions **1–6**, look at the description of what the teacher is saying and/or doing. Then read the areas of classroom management **A–C**. Which area does it match? Choose **A–C**.

---

1 The teacher says: *OK. We have just two or three more minutes of today's lesson. Today's jobs are: Tiger Team, please tidy the readers in the book corner; Crocodile Team, please put away all the materials and toys; Hippo Team, please shut down the computer. Then, everyone please check you haven't forgotten anything and line up by the door. Are you ready?*
Area of classroom management: The teacher is…

   A   checking understanding.
   B   using routines to develop responsible behaviour.
   C   using pair, group and whole class work.

2 The teacher stands in the middle of the classroom with their finger held up to their lips, saying nothing. The teacher looks at the children and waits until they are all quiet. Then the teacher says: *Good! Now listen carefully…*
Area of classroom management: The teacher is…

   A   using indirect correction.
   B   checking understanding.
   C   getting and keeping children's attention.

3 Children take a card from a mixed set. The teacher says: *Who has an animal on their card? Hold it up. OK, you are the Animal group. Who has some food on their card? Show me. Good, you are the Food group…*
Area of classroom management: The teacher is…

   A   setting up pair or groupwork.
   B   managing challenging behaviour.
   C   using routines to help children feel secure.

4 The teacher says: *Ana, Luis, please look at the poster. Do you remember, we agreed that we will be kind to each other at all times? Ana, were you kind to Luis then?*
Area of classroom management: The teacher is…

   A   using negotiated classroom rules to manage inappropriate behaviour.
   B   getting and keeping children's attention.
   C   using routines to develop responsible behaviour.

5 The teacher says: *Yes! It's 'arm'. Mika, show me your arm. Good!*
Area of classroom management: The teacher is…

   A   correcting language.
   B   checking understanding.
   C   rewarding positive behaviour.

6 The teacher says: *Mei, could you help me collect all the cards, please?*
Area of classroom management: The teacher is…

   A   using individual work.
   B   giving children practical responsibilities.
   C   giving positive feedback.

Reflection on learning in Part 3

You have come to the end of Part 3. This part of *The TKT Course: Young Learner Module* aimed to deepen your awareness and skills relating to teaching young learners in the classroom. You explored scaffolding strategies, practice activities and areas of classroom management. This part of *The TKT Course: Young Learner Module* also supported your knowledge and skills in preparation for the third part of the TKT: YL Module test: *Teaching Young Learners*.

Look back to the introduction to Part 3. You assessed your level of understanding before beginning the unit. Re-assess your understanding in each area.

You also identified questions or areas to find out about in each unit. How well do you think you have achieved these? What can you do to better achieve those you need to work on? For example:
- Re-read a section of the unit(s).
- Re-do or do more exploration activities (Second C of each unit).
- Discuss the unit(s) content with other teachers in your school or network.
- Re-do the TKT: YL practice task(s).
- Look in the *TKT glossary* or the glossary in this book to check meanings of key terms and concepts you are unsure about.
- Reflect on your classroom teaching more closely.
- Look for other readings or resources on the topic(s).

Write yourself two or three objectives for further learning and development in your TKT: YL PD Journal.

■ References and further recommended reading

PART 3 REFERENCES

Cameron, L. (2001). *Teaching Languages to Young Learners*. Cambridge: Cambridge University Press & Assessment.

Harmer, J. (2007). *How to Teach English.* (New Ed.) Harlow: Pearson Longman.

Lightbown, P. and Spada, N. (2021). *How Languages are Learned*. (5th Ed) [ebook] Oxford University Press

Robinson, A. and Saxby, K. (2015). *Fun for Starters: Additional Resources for Teachers Third Edition*. Cambridge: Cambridge University Press & Assessment

Pinter, A (2006). *Teaching Young Language Learners*. Oxford: Oxford University Press

Puchta, H., Lewis-Jones, P., Gerngross, G. and Zgouras, C. (2022). *Super Minds 2nd Edition*: *Level 3 Workbook*. Cambridge: Cambridge University Press & Assessment

RECOMMENDED FURTHER READING

Moon, J. (2000). *Children Learning English: A Guidebook for English Language Teachers.* Oxford: Macmillan. (Chapter 4)

Slattery, M. and Willis, J. (2001). *English for Primary Teachers. A Handbook of Activities and Classroom Language.* Oxford: Oxford University Press.

Part 4 | Assessing young learner learning in the classroom

Introduction to Part 4

Part 4 will help you understand and use formative, classroom-based assessment activities to monitor and assess progress and achievement of learning. You will deepen your knowledge about purposes and focuses of different assessment strategies and think about ways in which teachers and learners may respond to the results of assessment. You will also consider ways in which we can assess learning and look in more detail at feedback given by teachers and learners. This part of *The TKT Course: Young Learner Module* will support your knowledge and skills in preparation for the fourth part of the TKT: YL module test: *Assessing Young Learners*. You can find more information in the *TKT: YL syllabus* in the module handbook, which is available online.

In the first unit of this part of the book, Unit 11, you'll think about the purposes of different assessment types in teaching and learning. First, you'll consider the use of the term 'assessment' and reflect on your interpretation of this term in response to reading about the formative assessment cycle. You'll then look at different types of assessment appropriate for use with young learners and then consider how these may serve different purposes in teaching and learning.

Unit 12 turns to the focus of assessment: what to assess. This will consider areas we can assess in addition to language and language skills. The unit then looks at techniques for assessing these different areas and focuses on assessing non-language skills in the young learner context.

In Unit 13, you will look in more detail at the outcomes of assessment and the kinds of actions teachers or learners could take as a result of assessment outcomes. In the first section, we look at different ways teachers might adjust teaching and learning, based on assessment evidence. Then there is a focus on oral and written feedback before a closer look at using peer feedback with young learners.

At the end of each unit, there is a series of activities which will extend your learning, thinking and understanding, and help you explore and relate the unit theme to your own classroom practice or teaching context. These are followed by a set of TKT: YL practice questions based on the unit theme. It is recommended that you use your TKT: YL PD Journal to keep and organise your notes.

In the same way as in Parts 1, 2 and 3, read the ***can-do statements*** before you begin the units in this part of the book and evaluate your own understanding and skills for each. After completing Part 4, return to these statements and re-assess yourself. From that, you can develop an action plan to continue focusing on any particular areas you feel necessary.

SELF-ASSESSMENT

Unit	Rate yourself from: 1 (*Limited or not at all*) to 5 (*This is a strength*)	Rating before Part 4	Rating after Part 4
11	*I can* identify several different purposes for assessing children's language learning		
12	*I can* use classroom-based activities to assess different areas of children's progress and achievement		
13	*I can* respond appropriately to assessment evidence in order to improve teaching and learning		

In your TKT: YL PD Journal, identify two or three questions or areas you'd like to know more about in each unit in Part 4. When you have finished Part 4, return to these to see if you have answered them. If you haven't, read around the topic using the recommended reading list at the end of this part of the book. You can also find many resources for teacher professional development online.

Unit 11   Why assess learning: What purposes do different types of classroom-based assessment have?

LEARNING OUTCOMES

By the end of this unit, you will…
KNOWLEDGE: know more about different purposes for various types of classroom-based assessment
SKILLS: be able to identify why teachers use particular classroom-based assessment techniques

■ Starter Question

Before you begin this unit, read the starter question and make some notes. Then read the commentary and compare it to your notes.

 What does the term 'assessment' mean to you?

COMMENTARY

Assessment is a key part of teaching and learning; it can be defined as: 'to discover, judge, or form an opinion on learners' ability, **achievement, proficiency** or progress either formally or informally' (*TKT Glossary*, p. 4).

There are several different kinds of assessment including **formal assessment**, such as testing, where we assess children individually on their skills and knowledge, and **informal assessment,** which is carried out without the teacher setting a test: teachers continually assess informally during regular classroom activities, as a part of their everyday classroom practice. This is also known as **classroom-based assessment**. It may involve the use of classroom activities the teacher uses specifically to assess children, so they are planned as assessed activities which the teacher may observe or collect students' **worksheets** from, or it may be through the use of strategies such as **monitoring, observing, concept checking, eliciting** and other kinds of questioning, which the teacher uses all the time to gain a sense of children's language and skills use. The teacher may plan these strategies in advance of the lesson, for example by scripting some questions to check understanding. We can see, therefore, that assessment can be anywhere from very formal to very informal, unplanned and unstructured.

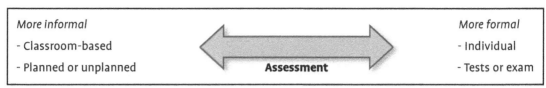

Figure 1: The assessment *formality* cline

Assessment may be done at the end of a period of learning, such as a term, course or even unit, in order to find out what was achieved, and not achieved. This is known as *summative assessment*; it is often formal. This is a final assessment **of** learning, so it does not influence future teaching and learning.

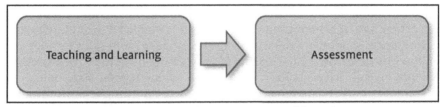

Figure 2: Summative assessment of learning

On the other hand, when assessment gives us information to help improve future teaching and learning, it is *formative assessment.* This is assessment **for** learning because we can use the assessment to improve teaching as well as learning. This kind of assessment usually happens in the classroom, so it is informal.

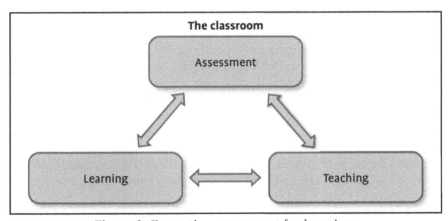

Figure 3: Formative assessment for learning

■ Key concepts

Reflect on the key concept question. Brainstorm your ideas, then expand your notes as you read.

 What kind of assessment can teachers use with young learners? **Note reasons for your answer.**

COMMENTARY

Children are still developing in different areas, including cognitively, physically, emotionally and socially, as well as developing in different skills such as *literacy*, **numeracy** and their *first language (L1)*. They are in a state of rapid change, and as we learned earlier, each child is unique in that development: they all develop from different starting points, in different areas at different times and different paces. This has implications for assessment, not least that we should assess regularly, with a focus on the *progress* they make, rather than assessing only at a single final point, that is, assessing overall *achievement*. This means we need to prioritise regular formative assessment (assessment *for* learning), even if we also assess summatively, as might be required in some contexts. If we break down learning into small steps, then we can assess achievement of these small steps, which will help us see progress overall. Therefore, it is important to be systematic and keep careful, regular records of performance, so we can see how children's language and skills develop over time. This allows us to see how each learner is progressing from their own starting point or level. To do this, we can collect information during regular classroom activities on an ongoing basis, as well as at several key moments during the term through more deliberate, planned, but still informally assessed tasks. This will help us give **feedback** to our learners on their progress and can show us when and how we need to support individuals, or even the whole class. This means that the results of the assessment can be used to shape our teaching and learners' learning, making assessment a central driver of the teaching and learning process.

Classroom-based assessment
Children perform best when working under normal conditions that they are familiar and comfortable with. They may work at their best when they are with their friends doing fun activities, which engage them and encourage them to use English in a meaningful **context**. These are the ideal situations to get an accurate picture of learners' abilities. If we ask children to sit a formal test, they will often feel stressed, nervous and even confused, especially as they are emotionally less mature than older children and adults. This will mean that many learners perform differently – often worse – than usual. So, when we assess children informally through a normal classroom task or activity, we will gain a better idea of what they are really able to do and, therefore, where they can go next in their learning. They will also be less impacted by the assessment emotionally and will probably enjoy the experience more.

Effective *classroom management* strategies can also give us information for assessment purposes. For example, a teacher who monitors carefully is constantly assessing their learners. Similarly, asking questions, nominating or eliciting from learners in the classroom gives teachers information about different learners' progress and achievement.

Self-assessment and peer assessment
Self-assessment is where children evaluate their own progress and achievement, while **peer assessment** is where they evaluate a classmate. Both of these assessment types ask children to use metacognitive and **higher order thinking skills**, which they may find challenging at first. However, when we regularly ask learners to use these kinds of assessment and give them guidance and support, they will begin to develop

these skills. We can therefore use these kinds of assessment to develop learning and cognitive strategies. Children can also gain a sense of ownership of their learning and start to appreciate each other as a resource to help them learn, so they become less dependent on the teacher. These kinds of assessment can be used in combination with or separate from teacher assessment to form an overall picture of either progress or achievement. We will find out more about self- and, in particular, peer assessment in Unit 13.

Portfolio assessment
Portfolios are an effective way to combine different types of assessment. A portfolio is a collection of learners' work done over time. The learners choose their best classroom work to showcase in different areas, so it is positive and fair as it focuses on what they can do well. This helps them analyse and understand their learning and to see progress over time. Children in the upper end of the age range can be asked to justify their choice of work, which strengthens the element of self-assessment.

Formal assessment
Sometimes learners may need or want to take a formal exam, for example to show their level of English (e.g. Cambridge Young Learners English Tests) or as a requirement in their school or even education system. Teachers can help learners to prepare for such tests using formative classroom-based assessment. The TKT Course: Young Learners Module focuses on classroom-based, informal assessment. For useful information on formal assessment and testing in the young learner context, see Papp (2019) and Hasselgreen and Caudwell (2016).

■ Key concepts and the YL classroom

Reflect on the *key concepts and the YL classroom* question. Brainstorm your ideas, then expand your notes as you read.

 What purposes can classroom-based assessment serve? **Note two or three ideas, then compare them to the following assessment purposes.**

COMMENTARY

We have seen that assessment is an integral part of the teaching and learning process. It is assessment which can drive learning forwards in a meaningful way for individual learners by helping us – and them – identify strengths and weaknesses and, therefore, plan next steps in learning. We may measure progress, for example by comparing ability in a specific language area with previous ability, or achievement, for example we can measure a learning **outcome** to see whether the learning objectives are met.

Assessment may be used for several different purposes for example:

To diagnose strengths and weaknesses
Just as a doctor examines a patient to make a diagnosis, using classroom-based assessment, we may want to get an idea of learners' current state, to find out where they need to improve, as well as to diagnose their strengths in language use, understanding, learning strategies and use of skills. This will let us plan or make

changes to our teaching and, through feedback, can show learners the next steps in their learning. This can help them in their journey towards achieving the **learning objectives** in a lesson or in a **syllabus** or to becoming better learners. We will also be able to identify children who need extra support or challenge in an aspect of their learning; we can see where to support all children so they can reach their potential in our classroom.

To identify children's likes and dislikes

We might also aim to find out information about children's **learning preferences**, their likes and their dislikes in relation to the kinds of classroom activities we ask them to do. We can gauge this through observation, or we can ask children directly what their preferences are. This will help us to tailor our teaching so that it is more appropriate, relevant and interesting to the children in our class.

To get feedback on our teaching

We can find out about our learners' perception of our lessons and our teaching, which can help us improve our practice by making it better suited to our learners' expectations. Where these expectations are not realistic, then we can talk openly with the learners and try to negotiate some kind of compromise. These may be related to the way we interact with learners, how we manage them in the classroom and the kinds of activities we use regularly. It ties together with identifying their likes and dislikes.

We may also gather feedback on the effectiveness of the **learning resources** and **materials**, classroom strategies and activities or **approach**. In addition, we may be able to use findings from classroom assessment of learning to tell us about this. This kind of evaluation might be organised by the school or institution and can involve different people in giving their opinions on the effectiveness and appropriacy of methodology.

To inform parents or caregivers about their child's progress and achievement

When we regularly collect and record information on each learner, it is easier to report to their homes meaningfully, for each learner. We are better able to give detailed individualised information about their performance, their progress and their achievement, for example in teacher-parent meetings, termly reports and other communications with parents and caregivers, such as through social media, an online learning management system or by email.

It is important that our assessment activity matches what we want to assess, and that it is fit-for-purpose. If our purpose is to identify children's achievement in listening skills and we ask them to write full, accurate responses to a listening task, then we are probably assessing writing more than listening. Similarly, if we ask children to work in groups to assess speaking skills, then we should keep in mind that a child may not feel confident to speak in a group setting, so it may not be fair to assess their speaking skills in this way.

■ Exploring the concepts in practice

FOLLOW-UP ACTIVITY *(see page 155 for answers)*

> **Read how a teacher uses a classroom-based assessment technique. Complete the task that follows.**

Following a sequence of lessons focusing on the topic '*In the town*', the teacher sets up a ***role-play*** activity, giving clear, supported instructions and modelling language carefully.

Children work in pairs to conduct the role play, using a ***language frame***.

The teacher walks around the classroom, listening and watching different pairs as they do the role play, assessing their use of the language previously taught and their speaking skills, as well as their ability to work effectively with each other in a pair. The teacher makes notes on areas children struggled with as well as what they did well.

When the children have finished the activity, the teacher asks them to think of two things they did well and one thing they could have done better. Some children share their feedback with the class, and the teacher asks if they enjoyed the role-play activity. The teacher notices how these compare to their own notes.

Then, the teacher gives feedback to the class, highlighting strengths as well as weaknesses, and explaining what they will do to work on these in the next lesson.

Identify the following purposes for assessment and mark them in the text:
1 Identifying children's achievement in the use of language and skills
2 Analysing children's use of learning strategies
3 Developing children's thinking skills through self-assessment
4 Diagnosing strengths and weaknesses
5 Identifying children's likes and dislikes
6 Moving learning forwards through assessment

REFLECTION

> **Look at the reflection questions below. Make notes of your answers in your TKT: YL PD Journal.**

1 In what way(s) has your view of assessment changed having completed this unit?
2 How would you respond to these teachers:
Teacher 1 says, '*I don't assess children in my classes because they find it too stressful. I just use one end-of-year test so that I can give them a grade for their report.*'

Teacher 2 says, *'The children keep online English portfolios. They upload their work when they feel proud of it. At the end of term, we review it and select their best.'*

Teacher 3 says, *'At the end of every class, I ask my children to review the lesson objectives and discuss whether they met them or not. Then I ask them which one(s) they will review at home'.*

3 If you are able to, meet with colleagues and discuss these scenarios.

 DISCOVERY ACTIVITY

Look at the discovery activities. Choose one or more to help you investigate your assessment practices in more detail.

1 Think about the kinds of assessments you use:
- assessment you used last year or term or..
- assessment you've used so far this year or term or..
- assessment you plan to use this year or term.

Make a note of your answers:
● What type(s) of assessment are there?
● Are they classroom-based?
● What are you assessing: progress or achievement?
● What is the purpose of your assessment?
● Does the assessment actually test what you want it to test?

2 Look up the term *assessment* in the *TKT Glossary*, where you can find different types of assessment. For each type, think about how suitable it is in your context:
- *What are some of the benefits of each type for you and your learners?*
- *Do you have any concerns about using this kind of assessment with children in general or with your learners specifically? What are they?*

3 Review the terminology you have encountered in this unit (such as formal-informal assessment; formative-summative assessment, portfolio etc.). Check your understanding of these by thinking of examples. If you feel you are unsure of the meaning of these words, follow up by expanding your reading. You can refer to the books listed at the end of Part 4, or you could look online at educational and/or ELT-related websites.

■ TKT: YL Practice task

 Do the practice task for this unit. Time yourself to see how long you take to answer all the questions. You should be aiming to complete it in six minutes or less.
Then check your answers in the answer key on page 158.

For questions **1–6**, read about assessment strategies. Choose the correct sentence **A–C**.

1 A teacher walks around the classroom to monitor children as they work in pairs. The teacher notes which learners are able to use the target language accurately.

    A   This teacher wants to assess progress in use of skills.

    B   This teacher wants to diagnose strengths and weaknesses.

    C   This teacher wants to assess achievement in use of language.

2 After an activity, the teacher asks the class of 6–7-year-old learners to put their thumbs up if they enjoyed the activity a lot, thumbs sideways if they quite enjoyed it and thumbs down if they didn't enjoy it.

    A   This teacher wants to assess achievement in use of language.

    B   This teacher wants to find out about children's learning preferences.

    C   This teacher wants to identify children who need extra support.

3 The teacher asks her 9–10-year-old learners to plan and draft writing in pairs before they write a final version. The teacher asks learners to hand in the plan, the first draft and final draft of their writing in order to see how they managed this process.

    A   This teacher wants children to assess their own learning strategies.

    B   This teacher wants to assess children's achievement in use of skills.

    C   This teacher wants to assess children's use of learning strategies.

4 The teacher sets up termly portfolio assessment with her class or 6–7-year-old learners. Learners choose samples of their best work in each skill to include in their portfolio. The teacher has a short interview with each learner to ask them why they chose each piece.

    A   The teacher wants to use self-assessment.

    B   The teacher wants to identify children's likes and dislikes.

    C   The teacher wants to identify achievement in the use of language.

5 The teacher observes learners as they work on classroom activities during the course and keeps brief, regular records on their performance in each skill. The teacher then uses these notes to write end of course reports to take home.

    A   This teacher wants to get information on learners' progress in order to give feedback to parents.

    B   This teacher wants to measure achievement of course learning objectives.

    C   This teacher wants learners to self-assess using a portfolio of their work in each skill.

6 The teacher sets a fairly formal test at the end of the course which aims to see how well learners have met the course learning objectives.

    A   This teacher wants to measure progress in use of language.

    B   This teacher wants to measure achievement in learning strategies.

    C   This teacher wants to measure achievement in use of language.

Unit 12 What to assess: What focuses do different types of classroom-based assessment have?

LEARNING OUTCOMES

By the end of this unit, you will...
KNOWLEDGE: be more aware of a range of focuses of classroom-based *assessment*
SKILLS: be able to select classroom-based assessment techniques appropriate to the focus of assessment

■ Starter Question

Before you begin this unit, read the starter question and make some notes. Then read the commentary and compare it to your notes.

 What can teachers assess in the young learner English classroom? Think of more than one possible focus of assessment.

COMMENTARY

Teachers of English may well feel it is their role to assess their learners' English – and it is, of course. However, we can and should assess more than just their English language in order to support the teaching and learning process.

Language and skills
We might want to assess learners' achievement or progress in their use of language through speaking and writing activities, where we can see their *productive* skills or their understanding of language through *receptive* skills activities, that is reading and listening. We may also assess the *subskills* of any of these four main skills, such as listening for specific information, *fluency*, *scanning*, use of punctuation, and so on.

> Example: Playing a card matching game where learners match picture *flashcards* with their word card assesses vocabulary knowledge and reading at word level.

Learning strategies
Similarly, we can assess children's use of or progress in *learning strategies*. Giving constructive *feedback* on their learning strategies will help them become better, more independent learners and, therefore, drive their learning forwards. Many of these skills are transferable to other school subjects, so can support them in their broader education and learning as well.

> Example: Reviewing and giving feedback on learners' vocabulary notebooks or learner-made picture dictionaries assesses this *learning strategy*.

Cognitive strategies

These are strategies which involve the use of thinking skills. As with many learning strategies, effective use of cognitive strategies not only supports learners' English language development, it also helps their development overall. We can assess and give feedback to learners on their use of such strategies or on their progress in them, and this allows them to develop further.

> Example: Playing 'What's missing?' (*'Kim's Game'*), where learners tell you what item you have secretly taken away from a scene or word from the board, assesses learners' memory as well as vocabulary knowledge.

Communication strategies

These are also life skills which have a particular impact on children's ability as learners of language. By assessing their communication strategies, we can give children valuable support in their development and help them understand how better to communicate with others in English.

> Example: Playing 'Happy Families' card game, where learners politely request cards from each other to make a thematic set, assesses the strategy of asking for an object. It also assesses language and vocabulary, as well as the cognitive strategy of categorisation.

It is always important to bear in mind that our assessment should match our *learning objectives*. If, through an activity, we are aiming to develop specific *target language* as well as a particular skill or strategy, then we can use this to assess in these areas. Look at this longer example:

> **Learning objective:** *To practise using greetings phrases in a role-play situation.*
> **Activity:** Learners collaborate to create, rehearse and present short dialogues using target language (greetings)
>
> *Here we might assess:*
> **Language:** the use of the specific phrases used (target language); but not other language used in the dialogue.
>
> **Skill:** Speaking and listening; but not their writing, if they write the dialogue.
>
> **Strategies:** How well the dialogue is performed (i.e. the learning strategy of rehearsing a dialogue to help memorise language); Use of appropriate language for greeting and responding to greetings (Communication strategy).
>
> We may also choose to assess their behaviour and interpersonal skills involved in collaboration.

■ Key concepts

Reflect on the *key concept* question. Brainstorm your ideas, then expand your notes as you read.

 How can we assess these areas? **Note one idea for each area given in the previous section.**

COMMENTARY

We saw in Unit 11 that *classroom-based assessment* is most appropriate for young learners of English. For this reason, teachers should ideally assess learners informally, when they are engaged in regular classroom activities. They can do this by *monitoring* and *observing* learners as they work in the classroom, then making notes on individuals' performance. This could be done using a checklist of objectives achieved or it could involve more informal notes on different learners, or be a combination of both. Teachers with large classes can focus on a small number of learners each time, which is easier than trying to assess all the class in one go.

If specific assessed tasks are needed, then these should also mirror those regular classroom activities, including the use of pair and group activities, so that learners are familiar with the activities and understand how they should be using language, skills and strategies in the activity. This will give a more accurate, truer picture of a learner's abilities, and learners will be less stressed and psychologically or emotionally impacted by assessment.

It is also helpful to collect learners' work, such as their *worksheets*, writing, pictures and so on, or to use a mobile phone to take photos of their work for assessment purposes. If appropriate permissions are obtained, videos could be made as learners work on speaking tasks, so they can be assessed later. Work can be marked in this way, with feedback given to learners in written form or even orally, as a video clip or voice message.

We also saw in Unit 11, that learners can be involved in assessment through *self- and peer assessment.* This helps them develop an understanding of the learning process and encourages them to reflect on their progress and plan future learning by setting their own goals and targets. This could be done using questionnaires after a lesson, theme or unit, where learners respond to simple *can-do statements* relating to the objectives. They can also identify what they need to do to improve on this kind of questionnaire. See Figure 2 for an example which could be used in conjunction with a review activity such as in Figure 1.

Figure 1: Review activity from Nixon and Tomlinson (2017) *Kid's Box* Level 1 Updated Second Edition, p.63: Cambridge University Press & Assessment

I can say the words in the game.	 😎	 🙂	 🙁	I need to _____
My friend can say the words in the game.	 😎	 🙂	 🙁	My friend needs to _____

Figure 2: An example self- and peer assessment form

*Learning **goals** and success criteria*

Learners can be involved in the assessment for learning process when we help them decide what they should and want to learn in an activity, lesson, theme or unit (learning goals), think about exactly what they need to have done (standards) to know they have achieved the goals (success criteria), then afterwards, by guiding them to reflect on what they did learn (self-assessment). This helps develop children's learning strategies and their awareness of the learning and language acquisition process, and supports them in becoming motivated, mature and independent learners. Look at these two examples of useful strategies we can use:

KWL

⇒ *What do you Know already?* Before learning, children **brainstorm** their current knowledge of language, topic and so on.

⇒ *What do you Want to know?* Also before learning, children set their own learning objectives based on what they are curious about. These could be content or language related.

⇒ *What did you Learn?* After the learning, children return to their objectives and decide how far they met them. At this stage, they can set new objectives for what they still want to know.

WALT and WILF

⇒ *WALT: We Are Learning To…*
The teacher and/or the learners express learning goals in terms of an activity, lesson, theme or unit, beforehand. They could be individual or for the whole class, such as on a wall display.

⇒ *WILF: What I'm Looking For…*
WILF accompanies WALT - success criteria are expressed as *what I'm looking for.*

For example:
WALT: *We are learning to write scary stories*
WILF: *I'm looking for at least five describing words to make the story scary*

This allows later assessment of learning by teacher and learners. In some activities, such as writing, WILF can be used as part of process writing, that is to help review, self-correct and re-draft writing. The teacher might hold a whole-class discussion about achievement of the goals after the learning, or learners may reflect this individually. The teacher can also use these goals and success criteria to assess learners. It may be beneficial to use learners' L1, if possible.

You can find out more about these kinds of strategy in Britton (2021).

Key concepts and the YL classroom

Reflect on the *key concepts and the YL classroom* question. Brainstorm your ideas, then expand your notes as you read.

 Why and how should teachers assess other non-language skills? **Note your ideas on this.**

COMMENTARY

In the Key Concepts section in this unit, we saw that learning, cognitive and communication strategies can be assessed in order to support learners in their development. Similarly, we can assess a number of non-language skills. These include affective non-language skills, or factors, and other life skills.

Affective non-language skills and factors

These include behaviour, ***motivation*** and ***attitude***, three areas which are closely related and sometimes difficult to separate. Learners' attitude towards learning English, towards the English-speaking community – at home or abroad – and towards learning in general will have an impact on their intrinsic motivation to learn English, that is the motivation that comes from within them. While many other factors are at play, motivation is a significant factor influencing children's behaviour in the classroom. All of these, therefore, impact on the success of teaching and learning of English and other learning. By assessing non-language skills, we can give feedback to learners and help them become more aware of and to develop these skills; we can also identify where we need to make changes to our teaching in order to better engage learners.

> Example: The teacher ***observes*** a group of learners in each lesson, and makes notes about non-language skills, such as: how well they co-operate with each other and work together; how carefully they listen in the classroom (e.g. to instructions); how quickly they get on task; how willing and careful they are with **at-home** tasks; and how appropriately they behave at different stages of the lesson.

Life skills

Life skills are the kinds of skill that people need and will need to operate in the world of today and tomorrow. The social nature of the language classroom is ideal for helping learners develop these skills, even if at a beginning level. We sometimes hear the term '21ˢᵗ Century Skills', which involve the '4Cs': Collaboration, Communication, Critical thinking and Creativity – skills which help children learn and which help to set them up for the future (for more on this, see Shin, et al., 2021). Cambridge University Press & Assessment's *Cambridge Life Competencies Framework* further outlines competencies in three broad areas: emotional development, digital literacy and subject knowledge, and gives a clear picture of how these skills develop at different stages of learning throughout life (see the Cambridge University Press & Assessment's website for a downloadable copy of the complete framework). We saw an example of assessing learning, cognitive and communication strategies and skills above; here, you can see an example of how we might assess digital literacy as part of classroom-based assessment.

> Example: Depending on children's age, the teacher might observe while learners use tools to interact with their device (e.g. the mouse, trackpad, touchscreen and/or keyboard, with older children) and keep records on their competences.
>
> It is also important to gain information on children's use of the online environment to ensure their safety and wellbeing online. We might do this by asking learners to keep a record of the sites they visit or clicks they make when researching for a mini project (this could be done using the browser history).

We have seen in this section that we should consider assessing more than just children's use and understanding of target language. In order to support children in their development and in their learning, we should focus on affective factors and life skills, which lets us give learners feedback and helps us and them to push their development forwards in these areas. By supporting learners with these skills, they will also become more effective language learners.

■ Exploring the concepts in practice

FOLLOW-UP ACTIVITY *(see pages 156–157 for answers)*

 Read about two classroom activities which could be used for assessing young learners. Think about what could be assessed in each activity and complete the table.

Step 1: Read about the assessed activities.

Assessed activity 1

Learners: 9–10 years old

Materials: Simplified local map using a grid, showing key roads, buildings, etc.

Activity procedure: Learners each have a map. They draw or mark their home on the map. Learners work in groups of four. They take turns to explain the location of their home to their group on the map, e.g. *My apartment is in the town centre. I live in the building between the bookshop and the convenience store.* The group members check their understanding by confirming the grid position, e.g. *Do you live in square D4?* Learners should draw or mark their friends' homes on their map.

Assessment procedure: The teacher monitors and observes two groups as they do the activity. The teacher uses a checklist to make records. The teacher collects the maps from these learners to compare and check they are the same.

Assessed activity 2

Learners: 6–7 years old

Materials: Realia or toy food items (several of each item)

Activity procedure: Learners sit in a circle. There are some food items (realia or toys) in the middle of the circle. The teacher asks learners to look and find which food they like best. They should take and hold that food item. The teacher **nominates** learners to tell the group about the food they have, e.g. *I've got a banana. It's a fruit. I love bananas.*

Assessment procedure: The teacher uses a checklist to record performance in various skills.

Step 2: What could the teacher assess in each activity? Put a tick or cross in the table. Make some notes relating to your answers.

	Assessed activity 1	Assessed activity 2
Speaking skills		
Listening skills		
Reading skills		
Writing skills		
Use of target language (grammar; vocabulary)		
Understanding of target language		
Communication strategies		
Learning strategies		
Cognitive strategies		
Affective non-language skills		
Life skills		

REFLECTION

 Arrange to meet colleagues or other teachers in network. Monitor and record your assessment practices. Share and discuss them together.

Work with some colleagues or teachers in your network.

First, keep an assessment diary for a period of time (e.g. one month). Note all the ways in which you assess learning in your classroom. Note the type, purpose and focus of these assessment activities.

Meet with other teachers (face-to-face or online). Share your diaries and discuss the assessment activities. You could think about:
- *How far do these activities give you a clear and accurate picture of learners' progress and achievement (individually or together as a set of assessment practices)?*
- *Overall, how effective were these activities as classroom-based assessment?*
- *Which of the assessment practices used by your colleagues do you want to use with your learners? Why?*

DISCOVERY ACTIVITY

> Follow the steps of the discovery activity, which is a mini research task focusing on learning goals and success criteria.

Step 1: Re-read the section on *Learning goals and success criteria*. Follow up on this topic by searching for techniques online or in books recommended here for Part 4. You could further investigate KWL, WALT and WILF or find other strategies.

Step 2: Plan to try out **one** of these strategies with one of your classes for a period of at least one month.

Step 3: Try out the strategy as it is recommended in your reading. Keep field notes of your observations and comments. You could use your TKT: YL PD Journal for this.

Step 4: Reflect on its success after a few tries using your field notes: *Do you need to make any changes to the strategy?* Perhaps your learners are very young and the process or wording need to be simpler. Perhaps the strategy will work better if learners do it individually, or together as a class. Make the changes to the strategy as appropriate.

Step 5: Continue to implement the strategy for the period, making more small adjustments as necessary, and continuing your note-keeping.

Step 6: Reflect again. Use your notes to help you reflect on the success of the strategy as you continue to try it. At the end of the trial period, talk to your learners about the strategy: *Did they understand why you were asking them to do this? Did they find it useful? Was it enjoyable? Would they like to continue doing it? Why?* Remember you can use learners' L1 if necessary and will need to grade your language and the concepts so they are appropriate to your learners' age and level. Make a final reflection.

You can use your TKT: YL PD Journal to record and keep track of your work. Remember to follow any ethical procedures required by your institution and to ensure you have informed consent of your learners and other participants before collecting any classroom data.

■ TKT: YL Practice task

> Do the practice task for this unit. Time yourself to see how long you take to answer all the questions. You should be aiming to complete it in seven minutes or less.
> Then check your answers in the answer key on page 158.

For questions **1–6**, read the statements about assessment strategies. Match each strategy to its main focus **A–E**. You can use a focus more than once.

Assessment focuses

A Learners' language

B Learners' use of cognitive strategies

C Learners' use of learning strategies

D Learners' use of communication strategies

E Learners' behaviour

Assessment strategies

1 Learners play a card game where they take a picture card. They tell their group what it is, e.g. *'duck'.* If they already have the same flashcard in their hand, they discard both and say *'ducks'.* If not, then they keep the card.

2 Learners work in a group of six to eight children. Each learner has a pencil sharpened to a different length. The teacher asks the children to stand in order, according to the length of their pencil.

3 The teacher gives learners a set of words which form a jumbled-up sentence. The teacher says the sentence; learners listen and reconstruct the sentence they have heard using the words.

4 The teacher asks learners to do a self-assessment activity at the end of the unit. They assess their achievement of the learning objectives of the unit as well as their participation in class, and say what they would like to do better in the next unit.

5 The teacher observes some learners while they work quietly on a writing activity. The teacher makes notes on learners' ability to work quietly without disturbing other children.

6 At the beginning of the term, the class and the teacher work together to make a poster showing useful expressions and functional language for communicating in the classroom. Each learner has a copy of the poster. When they use any of the language, they can tick it off. Around the middle of the term, the teacher asks the learners what they have used and what they haven't used yet.

Unit 13　Responding to assessment: How can I act on the results of classroom-based assessment?

LEARNING OUTCOMES

By the end of this unit, you will…
KNOWLEDGE: have found out about ways teachers and learners may respond to classroom-based assessment findings
SKILLS: be able to better implement appropriate adjustments and give formative feedback based on the results of assessment

■ Starter Question

Before you begin this unit, read the starter question and make some notes. Then read the commentary and compare it to your notes.

 What do/might you do after assessment? **Think about how assessment impacts on teaching and learning in your classroom. Note three or four points.**

COMMENTARY

In Unit 11, we saw how *assessment* for learning drives teaching and learning forwards as a result of the information it can give teachers and learners. This information is sometimes known as *'assessment evidence'*, and it can be used to make changes to teaching and learning and to set new learning *goals*. It might be evidenced in the teacher's notes from *observing* learners as they work on different activities, learners' *worksheets*, *coursebook* exercises, or written work, and so on.

There are a number of different areas we might consider changing in our classroom, based on what we find in that assessment evidence. For example, we may decide to review learning:

> Example: The teacher sees that learners have not achieved the learning they wanted them to (as per the learning objectives), decide that learners need more practice in that particular language area or skill, and then plan to review that area in an upcoming lesson.

> Example: The teacher notices from our monitoring and observation that several learners have difficulty with the pronunciation of one or two words in the unit vocabulary, so decides to review or even re-teach the pronunciation by giving extra models and playing a speaking game which focuses on *discriminating sounds*.

The teacher may decide to change the pace or to skip course content:

> Example: The closing stage of the lesson shows the teacher that learners have excelled and have achieved *learning outcomes* earlier than expected. The teacher decides to skip some upcoming activities or sections in the course plan or coursebook which give more practice in that area.

Teachers might also make adjustments to their planning and practice for a class, based on assessment evidence. They may make adjustments to the type of activity, for example:

> Example: The teacher adds support with *TPR (Total Physical Response)* to help learners understand and remember action verbs or key vocabulary in a *chant*.
>
> Example: The teacher simplifies the task demands of a writing activity (e.g. the amount of content or the number of words) when learners were not able to write in as much detail or length as required.

Adjustments may also be made to teaching materials or resources:

> Example: A text proved too challenging for learners, so the teacher repeated the activity using a simplified version of the text.

Another area teachers may decide to modify in response to assessment is classroom management:

> Example: Learners didn't perform very well because they didn't participate equally in an assessed groupwork activity, so the teacher decided to adjust and re-do the activity so that they are working in pairs.
>
> Example: Learners got over-enthusiastic and used too much *L1* in an assessed speaking game, so the teacher decided to set some parameters (rules) about use of language and made sure learners had a *settling* activity before the next similar activity.

Finally, another area of *classroom management* which may need adjusting is time: this may be to increase or decrease time given for an activity or it could be *wait time*, in the case where learners seem unable to respond to a question:

> Example: The teacher asked a series of similar questions. He noticed that only the stronger students in the class were able to respond, so he decided to wait a few seconds longer between asking the question and providing a prompt or reformulate the question to help the learner answer.

Teachers can respond to assessment evidence by making changes to how they teach the whole class, but assessment can also give us evidence to help make changes to how we teach or manage individual learners in the class. This doesn't necessarily mean making several substantial adjustments for each learner in the class like those mentioned above; we may make simple adjustments to help individuals, such as:

- changing the types of question we ask different learners to challenge or support them
- *monitoring* particular learners more closely to give them support or to manage their behaviour or interactions
- avoiding or preferring particular pairings or groupings
- giving additional activities to challenge **fast finishers** and extra practice to those who continue to have difficulty meeting *learning objectives*.

We can see, then, that the teacher can make small adjustments to their planning and classroom practice, based on the learners' response to and performance in activities. This kind of assessment for learning has a central role in developing effective classroom practice which supports all learners in their learning. A teacher who is constantly aware of how each learner in the class is performing can make their classroom more learning-oriented and help build the self-esteem of their learners. A key element in this process is *feedback*. We will look at this in the next section.

■ Key concepts

> Reflect on the *key concept* question. Brainstorm your ideas, then expand your notes as you read.
>
> *When and how do/could you give feedback to your learners?* **Make some notes, read the commentary and expand your notes.**

COMMENTARY

One of the most common ways to react to assessment evidence is to give feedback. This could be oral or it could be written. It might even be non-verbal, such as the use of *gestures*, like giving a thumbs-up. Feedback could be given by the teacher, other learners (peers) or by the learner whose work is being assessed (self).

The *TKT Glossary* reminds us on page 16 that there are three angles to feedback. The first two of these are relevant to this unit:

1 *To tell someone how well they are doing. After a test, or at a certain point in the course, teachers might give learners feedback on how well they are doing.*
2 *Teachers also give feedback after an exercise that learners have just completed; e.g. after learners have done a **gap-fill activity** the teacher conducts feedback by asking learners to tell him/her which words they have put in the gaps. He/she writes the correct answers on the board.*

Note that feedback should follow an assessed activity as well as regular classroom activities; it should also be given periodically to tell learners about their progress more generally. All such feedback contributes to the teaching-learning-assessment cycle of assessment for learning (see Unit 11) as they help to improve and push learning forwards.

For any feedback to help learners move forwards, it needs to be **formative**. This means it needs to give more than a score, grade or a simple but empty 'Well done!'. Teacher-to-learner feedback should recognise *what* the learner did well and *point forward* to the next step in learning. It should always use positive language and be worded and delivered sensitively and with care, as negatively perceived feedback can be very damaging to children's self-esteem and **motivation**.

Marks, scores, grades and comments

Often, teachers collect learners' written work, including artwork, **project** work, posters and so on, and will *mark, grade* or *correct* it. Giving just a score, grade or mark (e.g. 6/10, 65%, or B), however, is not helpful; nor is covering the learner's work with red pen corrections. The learner needs to know what they did well and what they did not do well so that they know what to focus on in their upcoming learning. They also need to know how they can improve: the feedback needs to be formative and realistic, that is it focuses on what learners are able to improve. Many teachers will have **observed** that young learners tend to look immediately at their mark at the top of a paper returned to them, and may likely ignore the written comments that are the formative feedback. It can be useful to give only comments; if grades or scores are essential, then they could be given later, separately. Allow time in class for learners to read their feedback, rather than having them put it straight away in their bags to be forgotten. This will encourage learners to read the feedback, so they are more likely to take it on board and, then, act on it. *'DIRT'*, Directed Improvement and Reflection Time, is a strategy whereby time is provided, usually at the beginning of a lesson, for learners to review and reflect on feedback they've been given, and to plan how to apply it in order to improve their work. Wiliam & Leahy (2015, Chapter 5) also discuss a number of studies on feedback strategies and outline a series of further useful techniques.

Feedback based on goals, success criteria and learning objectives

Through a process of goal-setting, where the success criteria are clear to the learner (see Unit 12), we can assess and give feedback specifically on the learner's progress towards those goals. See Petty's (2009, Chapter 6) 'Medals and Missions' feedback model for a useful example of how to structure formative feedback.

Similarly, if our learning objectives are related to content (what) or strategies (how), as well as language, then our feedback should be tuned to those as well. Even where our objectives are related to skills (such as in a writing activity, where learners write an email to a friend, or annotate a comic), we can comment on ideas as well as language.

Sensitive feedback: Even Better If…

The acronym *EBI* (Even Better If) reminds us to use positive, sensitive language when giving constructive feedback. For example, we may give balanced feedback such as: *'You answered all the questions in detail. Your work will be even better if you write neatly and check your spelling carefully.'* Indeed, feedback often involves us saying what a learner did not do well, and in order to help push learning forwards, we need to focus on areas that the learner needs to improve. We need to be sensitive when expressing this kind of feedback so that learners do not feel demotivated. It should focus on what can be done in future to help improve, that is, it should be forwards-pointing (e.g. *Next time, use an online or physical dictionary to check the spelling of words you aren't sure of; Try to spend a little longer on the activities and check your work before you hand it in.*). This will help ensure it is not phrased negatively (e.g. *Your spelling is not very good; You didn't try hard enough*). In this way, learners also begin to realise that we can learn a great deal from mistakes, that mistakes are part of the learning process.

Children in particular may be concerned about how they appear in front of their classmates. It is important to deliver individual feedback quietly and privately to avoid any feelings of embarrassment or fear. Regular self- and **peer assessment** can help learners get used to giving and receiving feedback and reduce these negative emotions, letting them feel more safe and secure in their learning environment.

Tips for giving feedback

We may give feedback orally, during the class for example, or in writing, on paper (or computer) based activities. Consider these tips:

Tips for effective oral feedback

✓ When giving individual feedback, try to do it *privately* and in a *quiet voice* when you are monitoring or, if in a whole class situation, encourage and prompt self-correction using positive language, facial expressions and gestures; balance the feedback, including praise for effort when relevant.

✓ Consider giving *delayed feedback* (i.e. not immediate), by taking notes of common mistakes as you monitor, then looking at those mistakes together as a class after the activity has finished, perhaps correcting them as part of a **whole-class** game or activity. This not only avoids interrupting learners doing an activity, but it also lets you anonymise the feedback.

✓ Remember to use a *positive tone* and *non-accusatory language* when giving feedback, so it is encouraging, even when you are drawing attention to something that can be improved.

✓ *Ask questions* to involve the learner in the feedback process, so it is two-way, rather than being directed from you. This will also allow you to know whether the learner can self-correct.

Tips for effective written feedback

✓ *Avoid using red pen*, which is aggressive and stands out more than the learners' writing.

✓ Write *legibly* and *intelligibly* so the child can read and understand your comments. You could give some of the feedback in their L1.

✓ You can use *stickers*, *stamps* and *emoticons* to make your feedback clear and child-friendly, but vary these so that they don't become equivalent to grades (e.g. A = very happy face; B = fairly happy face, etc.)

✓ *Avoid correcting all the mistakes*. Encourage **self-correction** of selected mistakes in target language using a simple error **correction code**.

✓ Respond to *content* (what they have written, their ideas, their illustrations) and effort, as well as language.

■ Key concepts and the YL classroom

> Reflect on the *key concepts and the YL classroom* question. Brainstorm your ideas, then expand your notes as you read.
>
> *Why and how might you involve learners in formative assessment and feedback?* **Think of at least one reason and two ways you do or could do this.**

COMMENTARY

As we have seen in this part of the book, *self-assessment* is where learners assess their own learning, while peer assessment is where they assess a classmate. Sometimes we might think that young learners are not very good at assessing themselves or giving effective feedback to others, but we can focus on developing these skills from an early age, in a simple way at first, then in a more sophisticated way as learners become more mature, gain more developed thinking skills, become better at interacting with others and better able to understand and reflect on the learning process.

There are many benefits to using self- and peer assessment. As we have seen already, both self- and peer assessment are very valuable learning strategies for English language learning and for other subjects, as well as being a life skill. Through developing these skills, children can become more independent and effective learners, who are better able to take responsibility for and manage their own learning. It allows them to have a voice in this process; this voice can be made stronger through involving them in setting their own goals and success criteria because they will understand where they are and where they are moving towards. Peer assessment in particular gives learners' work an audience, someone to appreciate it, which is especially important in large classes where the teacher might not be able to see and assess all the work of every child. It also helps learners to develop respect for each other, improve their social and communication skills, and to learn to receive feedback and accept failure or criticism.

In this section, we will look in more detail at peer assessment. Peer assessment and feedback can happen in a structured way, or it might happen less formally as learners work collaboratively in *pairs* or groups. If young learners are unskilled or insensitive when giving feedback to each other, it can be quite upsetting for the receiver of the feedback. It is very important, therefore, to help learners become skilled givers (and receivers) of feedback. We can do this by:

1 Spending time talking to learners about the importance of being kind and sensitive when giving feedback to each other. Agree on rules for giving feedback (e.g. *Make sure your comments are kind. Make sure you are giving ideas to improve.*) and focus on accepting feedback. You could do this in learners' L1.

2 *Scaffolding*: Provide a form, worksheet or feedback model (see below) to help learners with language and structure.

3 Scaffolding: Provide language for feedback. You could brainstorm some useful expressions and phrases, then put them on a classroom poster or on a feedback support sheet, or you could give learners a *language frame* to use.

4 Scaffolding: Provide a model of good feedback by using the same feedback model or tool that the learners use.

5 Feed back on feedback: Have learners to reflect and report on the *peer feedback* process so that they can develop their skills over time.

6 Start simple and actively develop skills over time, based on step 5 and on your own modelling. Learners will need that time to develop effective feedback skills.

There are a number of models for peer assessment, for example *Two stars and a wish:* In this model, learners are asked to give feedback which has two positive points (stars) and one constructive point (a wish), expressed in positive, non-accusatory language. The feedback can be guided in this way to help learners develop skills, for example they complete a feedback form:

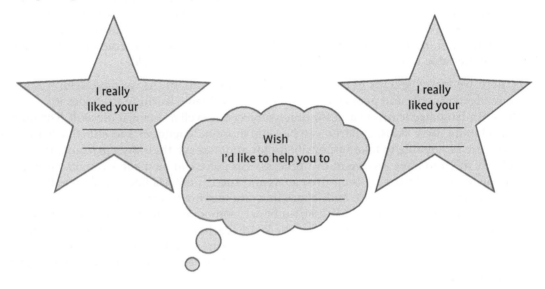

Figure 1: Two Stars and a Wish

Additional strategies to consider include:

Sharing success: Learners find a quote or a point that they like in their partner's work and share this with the class. It could be on a ***collaborative*** document online or put on a poster.

The sandwich model: In this model, constructive feedback is the sandwich filler, and positive comments are the bread. A series of feedback statements start with something positive, then move to a comment on what could be improved (and how), and finish up with another positive comment, leaving receiver on a high note. Learners could fill in a diagram of a sandwich with their feedback on a worksheet.

The feedback burger: It is similar to the sandwich, but the burger has four layers: The first is initial praise (the bottom burger bun), then the second is correction (the meat or veggie patty), the third is a suggestion (the lettuce), and finally the big bun on the top represents more praise. Written feedback can be presented in the form of a burger (Shin, Savić and Machida, 2021, p. 70).

Use of stickers: Learners put small stickers next to the part they would like to feed back on. The image or words on the stickers represents the kind of feedback being given (e.g. a heart for something great, an inquisitive emoticon for something to think about or work on). You could use stamps or drawings, which would be cheaper and more ecological than stickers. The learner will need to explain the feedback to their partner, in order for it to be formative.

Many of these, and other strategies for peer feedback can also be adapted for use in self-assessment, and some are already borrowed from teacher assessment strategies. If we can align self-assessment, peer and teacher assessment and feedback, then the messages will be clear and consistent, and learners will be able to develop these skills more rapidly and effectively.

■ Exploring the concepts in practice

FOLLOW-UP ACTIVITY *(see page 157 for answers)*

 Read the examples of teacher written feedback. Consider how effective they are and how they might be improved.

1 Fantastic, Yen!	2 You need to try harder.
3 Beautiful, neat work, especially the diagram.	4 Next time, check your spelling.
5 Can you write more about the animals in your story? Are they friendly? Scary? How do they move?	6 You gave a very detailed description of the scene. To improve your work, try to include all the key words. Look back and check the list to see which ones you left out.
7 34%	8 How did he feel? How do you know?
9 ☺	10 Your work has improved a lot, Dani. Be careful with 'a' and 'the'. I can see you are trying hard – well done!

REFLECTION

 Follow the steps of the KWL procedure to guide you in a mini research task.

Identify one or two areas from this unit which you would like to find out more about. Follow a KWL model to guide your research. Make notes:

K	*What do you already **Know** about the area?*
	Review the unit and make notes. Add points you already knew as well, if relevant. You could create a mind map, for example.

W	What do you **Want** to know about it?
	Write some detailed and precise research questions to guide you. You might want to know about the place of this area in the teaching-learning-assessment cycle, or you might want to know more practical suggestions to help you implement it. Find sources of information online or use the bibliography for this part to help you find useful resources. Make notes as you read.
L	What did you **Learn**?
	After you have researched, try to answer your research questions. Do you still need or want to find out more?

You could share what you have learned with teachers in your context or institution.

DISCOVERY ACTIVITY

Look at the three discovery activities to explore teaching and learning in your context. Choose one or more which are most useful in your context.

1 Keep an assessment diary where you track the assessments you use with one of your classes, the results of it and the adjustments you make based on those results (e.g. review, an area of classroom management, task types, teaching materials). If you already keep assessment records, you could add a section to those records where you note the adjustments, or you could create a table such as:

Date	Class	Assessed activity	Notes (findings)	Adjustment made
12/06/23	Tiger class	Pairwork activity (giving directions)	Jelena & Teo: co-operated well; struggled to use prepositions (TL) accurately;	Review prepositions with a game next lesson

2 Investigate your feedback:

A: Look back at examples of written feedback you have given learners in the past, e.g. written work you have marked or reports you have written for parents.

How formative is your feedback? How can you improve it?

B: Record yourself giving oral feedback to learners (Don't forget to check your school policy and to seek informed consent or permission for this from the school, parents/caregivers and students as necessary). You can use your mobile phone for this quite easily.

After the lesson, review the recording and analyse your feedback.

How formative is your feedback? How can you improve it?

Write some goals for your own development of feedback skills.

3 Experiment with self- and peer assessment models.

A: Review the various feedback models for self- and peer assessment introduced in this unit. Identify one or two which look interesting and relevant. Research them further online and plan to implement them in your lessons several times.

B: Record or keep detailed notes on the feedback your students give themselves and each other.

C: Analyse your notes to see how effective the technique has been.

D: Think about how it might be modified to be more effective for your learners and try it out again.

■ TKT: YL Practice task

 Do the practice task for this unit. Time yourself to see how long you take to answer all the questions. You should be aiming to complete it in seven minutes or less.
Then check your answers in the answer key on page 158.

For questions **1–6**, read about the responses to assessment. Match each response to its type by choosing the correct statement **A–C**.

1 *'Some learners were very noisy when they worked in same-gender pairs (boys with boys, girls with girls). So, I decided to mix boys and girls for the next pair-work activity.'*

   A   This teacher adjusted the task type.
   B   This teacher adjusted classroom management.
   C   This teacher adjusted the pace of learning.

2 *'All of the learners in the class could easily finish the exercise in the coursebook. I could see they understood and could use the target language really well, so I decided to skip the end of the unit and start the next one.'*

   A   This teacher adjusted learning objectives.
   B   This teacher gave learners oral feedback.
   C   This teacher adjusted the task type.

3 *'I usually add a funny stamp to the place in learners' work which needs attention. Then I put sandwich style feedback at the end of their work – the filling of the sandwich relates to that stamp.'*

   A   This teacher used oral feedback.
   B   This teacher used peer feedback.
   C   This teacher used written feedback.

4 *'I noticed that several learners in the class had difficulty reading the words on the flashcards, so I decided to add pictures to the words written in their coursebook so they could understand them better.'*

   A   This teacher adjusted teaching materials.
   B   This teacher reviewed learning areas.
   C   This teacher gave written feedback.

5   *'Three learners in my class of six were having problems remembering the target language form in the previous lesson. I decided to add an activity to the next lesson where they had to work in pairs to create a sentence jigsaw (containing the target language) for another pair to solve.'*

   A   This teacher adjusted the time spent on activities.

   B   This teacher gave feedback to pairs.

   C   This teacher reviewed learning.

6   *'My learners reviewed their at-home writing task in pairs and prepared a star or heart-shaped badge for their partner. On the badge they completed the sentence: 'Hi! My name is _____ . I'm good at ____.' On the back of the badge, they completed the sentence 'Next time, I need to _____.' Then they awarded their partner with the badge.'*

   A   This teacher gave written formative feedback.

   B   These learners self-assessed and gave written feedback.

   C   These learners peer assessed and gave written feedback.

Reflection on learning in Part 4

You have come to the end of Part 4. This part of *The TKT Course: Young Learner Module* aimed to deepen your awareness and skills relating to assessing young learner learning through classroom-based assessment. You explored purposes of assessing learning, focuses of assessing learning and ways teachers and learners may act on assessment evidence, including feedback.

This part of *The TKT Course: Young Learner Module* also aimed to support your knowledge and skills in preparation for the fourth part of the TKT: YL module test: *Assessing Young Learners.*

Look back to the introduction to Part 4. You assessed your level of understanding before beginning the unit. Re-assess your understanding in each area.

You also wrote two or three questions or areas to find out about in each unit. How well do you think you have answered these? What can you do to better achieve those you need to work on? For example:
- Re-read a section of the unit(s)
- Re-do or do more exploration activities (Second C of each unit).
- Discuss the unit(s) content with other teachers in your school or network.
- Re-do the TKT: YL practice task(s)
- Look in the *TKT glossary* or the glossary in this book to check meanings of key terms and concepts.
- Reflect on your classroom teaching more closely.
- Look for other readings or resources on the topic(s).

Write yourself two or three objectives for further learning and development in your TKT: YL PD Journal.

■ References and further recommended reading

PART 4 REFERENCES

Britton, M. (2021). *Assessment for Learning in Primary Language Learning and Teaching.* Bristol: Multilingual Matters.

Hasselgreen, A. and Caudwell, G. (2016). *Assessing the Language of Young Learners.* London: British Council.

Nixon, C. and Tomlinson, M. (2017). *Kid's Box. Level 1.* Updated second edition. Cambridge: Cambridge University Press & Assessment.

Papp, S. (2019). Assessment of Young English Language Learners. In *The Routledge Handbook of Teaching English to Young Learners.* S. Garton & F. Copland (Eds.). Pp. 389-407. London: Routledge.

Petty, G. (2009). *Teaching Today. A Practical Guide*. (4th edition). Cheltenham: Nelson Thornes.

Shin, J. K., Savić, V. and Machida, T. (2021). *The 6 Principles for Exemplary Teaching of English Learners*. Alexandria: TESOL International Association.

Wiliam, D. and Leahy, S. (2015). *Embedding Formative Assessment*. West Palm Beach: Learning Sciences International.

RECOMMENDED FURTHER READING

Cameron, L. (2001). *Teaching Languages to Young Learners*. Cambridge: Cambridge University Press & Assessment.

Ellis, G. and Ibrahim, N. (2015). *Teaching Children How to Learn*. Peaslake: DELTA Publishing.

Fisher, R. (2005). *Teaching Children to Learn*. Cheltenham: Nelson Thornes.

McKay, P. (2006). *Assessing Young Language Learners*. Cambridge: Cambridge University Press & Assessment.

Petty, G. (2014). *Teaching Today. A Practical Guide*. (5th edition). Oxford: Oxford University Press.

Follow-up activities: Answer keys and commentaries

UNIT 1

A **True:** The activity includes TPR (physical), various thinking skills (cognitive), interacting in pairs and collaborating to plan and conduct a survey (social).

B **True:** Children work individually when surveying family or friends and reporting on the data; they work in pairs to practise the language; they work in groups to conduct the survey.

C **True:** They first listen to the story and do the actions. Then they practise the language in pairs, before creating their own survey questions.

D **True:** The example of a chunk here is *What time do you…?* Children add the verb to this chunk to create the survey questions.

E **False:** This is not a classroom routine.

F **True:** Many daily routines are carried out at home (e.g. get up, brush your teeth); children read a story, which may be a home activity; they are asked to survey their family or friends and report on this as part of their findings.

G **False:** Depending on the story or media you choose, it can be very suitable for children in either the younger end or upper end of the 6–12 years age range. Similarly, younger children can present their findings in a very simple way, whereas older children in the age range can work with more advanced data presentation techniques such as a more complex table or maths concepts, e.g. percentages. The teacher will need to model and give support to children of all ages in using the computer to create tables, print and stick; a template may be useful.

UNIT 2

1 **D:** It is important to explain the reasons behind some of our classroom practices to parents or caregivers, so that they will support us and their children in their learning.

2 **B:** A person who has a growth mindset views learning as a series of small, achievable steps which will lead the person to achieving a bigger goal.

3 **A:** We don't always need to add in extras to our lessons, we can often adapt the material we are asked to use. We will look more at this in Part 2 of this book. Answer C would also be a possibility here as it is an example of the kind of learning strategy learners could reflect on.

4 **F:** Children can learn a great deal from each other; it is important to remember too, that children's level of language does not indicate the same level of ability to use learning strategies.

5 **C:** The Plan – Do – Review model can easily be incorporated into a lesson without taking up extra time or requiring supplementary materials.

6 **E:** Children will improve at self-assessment the more they do it. Over time, they will be able to reflect more effectively on what and how much they have learned. We will look at related ideas in Part 4 of this book.

UNIT 3

Extract 1) B; D; E. In part 1, learners predict the content of the texts, based on the images; They will need to skim read the article (read it quickly) to check their answers to the questions in part 1. They are directed to find specific words in the text and work out what they mean, based on the context.

Extract 2) A; B; F. On the second listening in activity 1, learners need to put the pictures in the correct order (sequence), based on what they heard. They may then scan the sentence options in activity two to find key words which match the stages in the story sequence and, therefore, specific items they can see in the pictures. Children create their own situations in Activity 3 and may also take risks with language, although they are not specifically encouraged to do so.

Follow-up activities: Answer keys and commentaries

UNIT 4

Communication strategy	Example	Game 1: Happy families	Game 2: Charades	Game 3: Hopscotch
Using gestures and body language to explain	Miming		✓ (This is a key part of this game)	
Congratulating a winner	*Well done!*	✓ (There is a winner who can be congratulated)	✓ (There is a winner who can be congratulated)	✓ (There is a winner who can be congratulated)
Turn-taking	*It's your turn!*	✓ (Learners take it in turn and can use language to communicate in order to manage this together)	✓ (Learners take it in turn and can use language to communicate in order to manage this together)	✓ (Learners take it in turn and can use language to communicate in order to manage this together)
Giving opinion	*I think it's…*		✓ (This is a guessing game, where learners give their ideas)	
Use of visuals	Using numbers; pictures	✓ (This relies on picture cards, although these could also be word cards for older children)		✓ (The hopscotch grid is a visual. It will also show numbers and can use pictures.)
Asking for something	*Could I have it, please?*	✓ (This is a key part of the game)		
Giving something	*Here you are!*	✓ (Learners can be encouraged to use a language strategy to communicate this)		
Collaborating	*Let's…*			✓ (This can be a collaborative game if played in pairs or small teams)

UNIT 5

1 Syllabus fit and previous learning
2 Learning outcomes
3 Learning resources
4 Possible problems and solutions
5 Personal teaching aim
6 Procedure
7 Interaction patterns
8 Assessment evidence
9 Differentiation
10 Lesson evaluation

UNIT 6

1) The teacher could do one or more of the following:
   – Omit one or more vocabulary items from the picture by covering them up or by displaying a modified version on a classroom screen.
   – Add more visual support using photos of landscapes in temperate climates which include some of these features. Elicit from the class what they can see and talk about the features which are less familiar.
   – Personalise the content by adding some questions after the activity: ask children which of these things they can see in their community or local area.
   – Add a game-like activity to pre-teach the potentially challenging vocabulary.

2) The teacher could do one or more of the following:
   – Simplify the language in the instructions and/or the project steps.
   – Prepare a set of control and experiment plants by doing the project in advance. This can be used as a model of the final product so children know what they are aiming at.
   – Add to the instructions by asking questions about the children in the pictures (e.g. What are they doing? What is in the cups?).
   – Use some of the children's own language to explain challenging key words of steps (e.g. vinegar). These words could be added to 'My Dictionary'.
   – Add a stage to the project to look at the final outcome of the experiment (this comes later in the material).

UNIT 7

Teacher 1: F and L
Teacher 2: D and E
Teacher 3: C and J
Teacher 4: I and K
Teacher 5: A and G
Teacher 6: B and H

UNIT 8
Question 1

1 **The teacher grades their language.** Yes. The teacher uses simple and clear language, although also tries to make it natural. We don't know how quickly or clearly they are speaking, however.

2 **The teacher repeats or rephrases their language.** Yes. There is repetition in 13, which is where the teacher is modelling the question form. There is rephrasing in 27, where the teacher uses *'hide'* and *'secret'* and in 25: *Who wants a turn?* [pause] *Who wants to play?*

3 **The teacher asks questions to check children's understanding.** Yes. The teacher checks understanding of the groupings and order of turns in 31.

4 **The teacher uses or has children use a language other than English.** No. We only see English in the transcript.

5 **The teacher corrects children's language in different ways.** Yes. The teacher elicits the correct singular form (*mouse*) when Kaya uses the plural form (*mouse*) in 17–24.

6 **Non-linguistic support.** Yes. The teacher uses a lot of gestures to support understanding of language and the procedure of the activity.

7 **Praise.** Yes. The teacher uses praise to show students they are correct using different expressions such as *'Well done!'* (7) and *'Very good!'* (27) and *Excellent!* (31).

8 **Contextualising language.** No, although the language is already contextualised in this game because it is a genuine guess.

9 **Preparing for an activity.** Yes. This is the main focus. In particular, the teacher provides clear oral models of language children will need in order to do the activity. The transcript shows the modelling of the activity students will do in groups by the teacher and by volunteer students.

10 **Using the senses.** Yes. The demonstration makes use of the sense of sight and hearing. Other senses are not necessarily used, although there is also movement and mime involved.

11 **Language support material**. No. There is no material used to support understanding or use in this example. Flashcards show students which animal they should mime.

12 **Managing interaction.** Yes. The teacher takes time to set up the groups and the order in which the students should take their turns when playing the game. They also check that students understand this. Note that the transcript opens with a short routine to help the teacher get students' attention before starting to model the activity. Students are sitting in a circle to help them focus and keep their attention.

Question 2

A The teacher's instructions are unnecessarily complex, using some language which may be difficult for all children in the class to understand. The instructions are poorly organised and lack coherent sequencing. Finally, the teacher does not demonstrate the activity and does not check students know what to do appropriately. Note that the question 'Do you understand?' is not a reliable way to find out if children know what to do – they may say or think they understand, but haven't, or they may just say yes, even if they don't!

Suggested improved instructions:

Teacher: *Look at the word puzzle.* (Shows the worksheet on the screen). *Some fruit words are hiding in the puzzle. Who can find a fruit word?*
Student: *Here! Orange.*
Teacher: *Yes! Well done, that's right. (…) OK, so please work with your partner. Find ten fruit words in the puzzle. (…) Who can tell me: How many words will you find?*
Students: *10!*
Teacher: *Yes. And what kind of words?*
Students: *Fruit!*

Teacher: *Exactly, well done. Please turn to your partner. You have 5 minutes, starting… now!* [Teacher sets timer on the computer].

B There are two concerns with this feedback: First, the feedback is imprecise, so students have no idea what they did well exactly. It is possible that there were aspects of their work which was not done as well as others, so students don't know what they have achieved and what they still need to work on. Secondly, the tone of the feedback may be friendly and encouraging, but is inappropriate. 'Guys' generally refer to boys and men, for example.

'Well done on your work, everyone! I could see you all tried your best, which is great! You all spoke really clearly and explained your pictures using the right words. Next time, try to do more to show you're listening to your partner. We're going to learn about this in our next lesson!'

C The explanation of the word by the teacher is unnecessarily complex – using higher level words than the word being explained! The teacher could simply say: *'We use it for cutting'*, and use mime or gestures to model using a knife. If the teacher has predicted this as a new word in the lesson when planning, they could show a flashcard, realia, or an image on the screen or, if not predicted, draw a simple picture on the board. The teacher can then drill the word and have children mime cutting with a knife as they say the word. The teacher may ask concept check questions, especially to check they haven't misunderstood the word to mean 'cut'. Note that giving the initial letter of the word is also very confusing, not only because the 'k' is silent, but also due to the age of the children, who are likely beginning literacy skills development.

D The feedback given by this teacher is confusing and inaccurate. This activity is probably a controlled practice activity, such as a drill, which has an accuracy focus. The teacher should, therefore, correct the children's language clearly and overtly. The teacher may use different techniques to do this, such as recast, reformulation, echo correction, elicitation and should have the learner repeat the correct sentence. For example:

Teacher:	*Yes, Mingze?* (shows a flashcard of a girl reading a book)
Mingze:	*She... er... reading book.*
Teacher:	*She mmm reading...*
Mingze:	*She is reading book?*
Teacher:	*Good. She's reading a book. (...) Say it again, Mingze?*
Mingze:	*She's reading a book.*

Teacher:	*Great, well done! She's reading a book. (...) Ok, now the next one. Yan? What's he doing?* (Teacher shows a flashcard of a boy riding a bike)
Yan:	*He read a bike.*
Teacher:	*Read? Is he reading?* (mimes reading) *Or riding?* (mimes riding)
Yan:	*Riding. He riding a bike.*
Teacher:	*OK. He's riding a bike. Yan?*
Yan:	*He's riding a bike.*
Teacher:	*That's right. Well done, Yan.*

UNIT 9
Extract 1

	1. Activity type	2. Practice	3. Category*	4. Demands**	5. Support
Activity 1 on p. 26	Gap-fill (letter fill) activity	Vocabulary (receptive and productive); Spelling.	Controlled	Cognitive: interpreting pictures; consider order of letters in words. Involvement: there are 9 words to write, which is quite a high number. Physical: Fine motor skills (drawing lines).	Letter prompts; Picture prompts
Activity 2 on p. 26	Short answer question	Reading; Writing (copying); Vocabulary (receptive)	Controlled	Cognitive: Uses words from Activity 1. Language: Need to read and understand clues (descriptions).	Picture prompts to choose from
Activity 3 on p. 26	Gap-fill (choose from options in a box)	Reading; Vocabulary (inducing set phrases/ chunks, word class); Writing (copying)	Controlled	Cognitive: Need to understand context from dialogue and picture. Language: Need to read dialogue carefully.	Options in a box; Picture to provide context for dialogue; Surrounding words and context of the text

153

Follow-up activities: Answer keys and commentaries

	1. Activity type	2. Practice	3. Category*	4. Demands**	5. Support
Activity 1 on p. 27	Gap-fill (choose from limited number of options)	Reading; Writing (copying); Grammar (past simple of the verb *to be*, positive and negative; Recognition of singular/ plural)	Controlled	Cognitive: Need to understand context from text and picture. Language: Need to read text carefully.	Pictures for context; Surrounding words in the text
Activity 2 on p. 27	Sentence completion	Writing at sentence level; Vocabulary (town words, prepositions of place); Grammar (use of *to be* in past simple)	Less controlled / freer	Cognitive: Need to understand context from pictures, including the concept of changes in time to the one place shown and, the need for past simple to talk about the left-hand picture.	Picture input; Decreasing sentence stems (note that this support is gradually removed)

*If we look at the activities, we can see that all the activities on p. 26 and activity 1 on p. 27 are tightly controlled. There is only one possible answer and there is no freedom for the learner to be creative with language. It would be difficult, therefore, to say which is more or less controlled. Activity 2 on p. 27, however, is freer because the learners can choose what to focus on in the picture and, therefore, what to write. However, this also limits the possibilities for the focus of their answers. The sentence stems also limit learners somewhat, but this is in order to elicit the past form of *to be*, which is the objective of the practice activity. Note that in later sentences, learners could be more creative, e.g. sentence 3, the learner could use a different verb such as *A long time ago, people fished in the river*; for sentence 6, the learner could write about 'now', if they wanted: *Now, there is a big supermarket carpark*. As such, this could be classed as 'less controlled' or 'freer'.

** Note there is no use of metalanguage to talk about grammar (e.g. *past simple*) in this extract.

As this extract comes from a workbook, these are all activities which are settlers and involve children in individual work.

Extract 2

- This is a very controlled practice activity.
  False: There is considerable freedom given to learners in terms of content and language. They are limited to a food topic, something they don't know well, but choose and research using specific web-based sources (note that we should always consider directing young learners to specific sources for research-based tasks, to encourage safe internet usage).
  The sentence frame is provided in the teacher's notes, but it is up to the teacher whether to restrict the learners to this language (see below).
- This activity practises past simple for describing condition, state and habits.
  False: It practises present simple.
- The teacher could support learners by providing a sentence frame such as in the third point shown. This would make the activity more controlled.
  True: As mentioned above, a frame is provided and the teacher can choose whether to give learners all or some of this frame to work from as a support. This could be done using a model poster that the teacher creates before the lesson.

- Learners practise mostly Speaking and Listening in this activity.
  False: Learners will practise some Speaking and Listening as they talk to each other and to the teacher when working on the activity, but the main objective of this activity is for Reading (from web-based material and each other's posters) and Writing (on the poster). The teacher could encourage the learners to draft and check their text before writing it on the poster, which will allow a process writing focus.
- Learners could work collaboratively in a group in this activity.
  True: This is an ideal activity for pair or group. Learners could be given or could choose roles to play in the group (or pair), such as researcher, scribe (writer), designer, manager, artist, and so on. This will encourage all learners to participate.

UNIT 10
1 C
2 A
3 B
4 D

UNIT 11

Following a sequence of lessons [1: *this suggests we are looking at achievement*] focusing on the topic 'in the town', the teacher sets up a role-play activity, giving clear, supported instructions and modelling language carefully.

Children work in pairs to conduct the **role play** [1: *the focus is on the speaking skill*], using a **language frame** [1: *the focus is also on language use*].

The teacher walks around the classroom, listening and watching different pairs as they do the role play, **assessing their use of the language previously taught and their speaking skills** [1: *the focus is on skills and language*], as well as their ability to work effectively with each other in a pair. The teacher makes notes on **areas children struggled with as well as what they did well** [4: *this is a diagnosis of strengths and weaknesses*].

When the children have finished the activity, the teacher **asks them to think of two things they did well and one thing they could have done better** [2, 3: *here children self-assess using a learning strategy*]. Some children share their feedback with the class, and **the teacher asks if they enjoyed the role-play activity** [5: *the teacher asks about likes and dislikes*]. The teacher notices how these compare to their own notes.

Then, the teacher gives feedback to the class, highlighting strengths as well as weaknesses, and explaining what they will do to work on these in the next lesson [6: *this moves the learning forwards*].

Follow-up activities: Answer keys and commentaries

UNIT 12

Assessed activity 1	
Speaking skills	Yes. Learners should tell their friends where their home is in the town; they also should ask to confirm the grid location. The teacher can also assess pronunciation.
Listening skills	Yes. Learners should listen to each other in order to complete their maps.
Reading skills	No. There is no reading required. To assess reading, the teacher could ask learners to prepare a short, written description of the location of their home, which they share with their group to read and follow.
Writing skills	No. There is no writing required. To assess writing, the teacher could ask learners to prepare a short, written description of the location of their home, which they share with their group to read and follow.
Use of target language (grammar; vocabulary)	Yes. The target language is likely to be prepositions of place, places in the town, question and answer forms. Learners need to use this accurately to achieve the task.
Understanding of target language	Yes. Learners need to understand the language mentioned above in order to locate their friends' homes.
Communication strategies	Yes. Learners may need to use strategies such as asking for clarification, repetition, thanking and so on.
Learning strategies	No. There are not really any learning strategies needed in this activity.
Cognitive strategies	Yes. Map skills involve several cognitive processes, including the grid system and other spatial skills.
Affective non-language skills	Yes. Learners need to co-operate and collaborate to work as a group; they all need to participate actively in order to complete the activity.
Life skills	Yes. Some life skills are already mentioned. In addition, the activity could be done using online maps to help assess digital skills. There may be some subject knowledge required (e.g. local geography).

Assessed activity 2	
Speaking skills	Yes. Learners' speaking skills are assessed when they use the target language. The teacher can also assess pronunciation.
Listening skills	Yes. The teacher can assess learners' understanding of the instructions.
Reading skills	No. There is no reading in this activity. The teacher could use word cards instead of items if they wanted to assess reading.
Writing skills	No. There is no writing in this activity. The teacher could ask learners to write labels for their food items to help assess writing at word level.

Use of target language (grammar; vocabulary)	Yes. The target language is the structures (*I've got a..; I like…; It's a…*) and the vocabulary for the food items and categories.
Understanding of target language	No. There are no receptive skills needed relating to the target language.
Communication strategies	No. There is no communication in this activity, although learners may need to use some communication strategies if they don't understand what to do, or need help.
Learning strategies	No. There are no learning strategies needed in this activity.
Cognitive strategies	Yes. Learners need to categorise the food item.
Affective non-language skills	Yes. The teacher can assess learners' behaviour, their motivation and other affective non-language skills. This can be easy to do when they are sitting in a circle because they are visible.
Life skills	No. There are not really any life skills involved in this activity.

UNIT 13

1 This feedback is positive and the learner may feel good as a result, but it doesn't tell the learner what was so good in their work. There is no comment on what to improve next time.

2 As with comment 1, this feedback has no detail. The learner doesn't know what they haven't done well at – perhaps they did try hard but were unable to succeed. They don't know. It is important to always find something positive to include in feedback.

3 There is positive feedback here and some detail, although it is limited. There is no comment on what to improve next time.

4 This feedback is forward-looking and includes a little detail, but does not include anything positive. It could be more specific – spelling of what?

5 This feedback is formative and helpful in that it suggests ways to improve the writing. There is no positive feedback here.

6 This feedback is detailed and formative. It is a good example of effective feedback.

7 This feedback is not helpful. The learner knows they did not do well at all, but has no idea what they did poorly for 66% of their work, or well for 34% of it! They don't know what or how to improve next time.

8 This feedback helps learners think critically and helps learners improve on their writing. There is no positive comment, however.

9 Teachers often use sets of stamps for giving their feedback or for peer feedback. This stamp shows the learner's work is adequate, but the learner does not know what was OK or how they can improve, to get the smiling stamp next time. A comment is needed alongside the stamp.

10 This feedback is presented as a sandwich, but it lacks detail. The teacher needs to explain how the learner's work has improved and what he is trying hard at in particular. The 'meat' in the sandwich is precise as it says where there is a problem with the learner's grammar, but the learner doesn't know exactly what the problem is or how they can improve it. Adding this detail might make the feedback more like a burger than a sandwich.

ANSWER KEY FOR TKT: YL PRACTICE TASKS

1	1	C	2	E	3	A	4	F	5	G	6	D
2	1	A	2	C	3	B	4	B	5	A	6	C
3	1	A	2	C	3	B	4	C	5	B	6	A
4	1	A	2	B	3	A	4	C	5	A	6	C
5	1	F	2	C	3	B	4	D	5	E	6	A
6	1	B	2	A	3	A	4	B	5	C	6	A
7	1	B	2	C	3	E	4	D	5	A	6	F
8	1	H	2	C	3	D	4	G	5	A	6	F
9	1	B	2	B	3	A	4	C	5	B	6	C
10	1	B	2	C	3	A	4	A	5	B	6	B
11	1	C	2	B	3	C	4	A	5	A	6	C
12	1	A	2	B	3	A	4	C	5	E	6	D
13	1	B	2	A	3	C	4	A	5	C	6	C

List of terms found in the *TKT Glossary*

Term/Unit	1	2	3	4	5	6	7	8	9	10	11	12	13
Accuracy									✓	✓			
Achievement					✓						✓		
Aim					✓								
Approach											✓		
Art and craft activity	✓						✓						
Assessment											✓	✓	✓
Attention span	✓								✓				
Attitude	✓	✓			✓							✓	
Authentic (materials)						✓	✓						
Brainstorm		✓		✓								✓	
Can-do statement	✓	✓			✓			✓				✓	
Chant	✓		✓			✓	✓		✓	✓			✓
Choral (drill)					✓				✓				
Chunk	✓			✓					✓				
Classroom-based assessment											✓	✓	
Classroom management	✓				✓					✓	✓		✓
CLIL (Content and Language Integrated Learning)	✓												
Closed question			✓					✓	✓	✓			
Collaborative/collaborate				✓		✓	✓		✓	✓			✓
Colloquial				✓									
Communicative (activity)	✓			✓		✓							
Concept check questions (CCQ)								✓					
Context	✓		✓		✓	✓	✓		✓	✓	✓		
Controlled (practice)									✓	✓			
Correction code													✓

List of terms found in the *TKT Glossary*

Term/Unit	1	2	3	4	5	6	7	8	9	10	11	12	13
Coursebook	✓	✓			✓	✓	✓		✓				✓
Curriculum		✓			✓	✓	✓						
Deduce			✓										
Dialogue			✓				✓						
Dictation									✓				
Differentiate			✓		✓			✓					
Discriminate (sounds)													
Drill								✓	✓				
Elicit				✓						✓	✓		
Extension activity						✓		✓					
Facial expression	✓			✓				✓					
Feedback			✓					✓		✓	✓	✓	✓
Finger correction													
First language (L1)	✓							✓			✓		
Fixed expression				✓									
Flashcard	✓				✓	✓	✓	✓				✓	
Fluency									✓	✓		✓	
Focus on form (FoF)									✓				
Focus on meaning (FoM)									✓				
Formal assessment											✓		
Formality				✓							✓		
Formative (assessment)								✓			✓		✓
Free practice									✓	✓			
Function/functional language				✓					✓				
Gap-fill									✓				✓
Gesture	✓			✓			✓	✓	✓	✓			✓
Goal		✓	✓						✓	✓		✓	✓
Grade (language)		✓								✓			
Graded reader		✓	✓			✓		✓	✓	✓			

Term/Unit	1	2	3	4	5	6	7	8	9	10	11	12	13
Handout					✓	✓							
Higher Order Thinking Skills (HOTS)			✓						✓				
Informal assessment											✓		
Information gap									✓				
Input	✓					✓			✓				
Interaction pattern	✓				✓	✓				✓			
Interactive whiteboard (IWB)					✓	✓	✓			✓			
Intonation	✓								✓				
Jigsaw (activity)						✓			✓				
L1 (First language)		✓		✓					✓				✓
Language frame									✓		✓		✓
Learning strategy		✓										✓	
Lesson plan		✓			✓			✓					
Learning preference(s)	✓										✓		
Lexical set				✓									
Literacy	✓					✓			✓		✓		
Model (v/n)				✓		✓	✓	✓	✓				
Monitor					✓	✓					✓	✓	✓
Motivation	✓	✓			✓			✓	✓			✓	✓
Mixed level/ability		✓									✓		
Nominate			✓									✓	
Objective		✓	✓		✓	✓			✓	✓	✓	✓	✓
Observe				✓		✓					✓	✓	✓
Open pairs									✓				
Open questions	✓		✓										
Outcome					✓			✓	✓		✓		
Pairs	✓	✓		✓				✓		✓			✓
Peer assessment											✓	✓	✓

List of terms found in the *TKT Glossary*

Term/Unit	1	2	3	4	5	6	7	8	9	10	11	12	13
Peer correction										✓			
Peer feedback				✓									✓
Personalisation						✓			✓				
Picture dictation									✓				
Plenary		✓								✓			
Portfolio (assessment)											✓		
Practice (activity)				✓					✓				
Pre-teach							✓	✓	✓	✓			
Predict	✓		✓				✓						
Problem-solving				✓			✓		✓				
Procedure					✓								
Productive	✓						✓		✓			✓	
Proficiency											✓		
Project		✓		✓	✓	✓	✓			✓			✓
Prop	✓						✓	✓					
Realia					✓	✓	✓	✓					
Recast								✓					
Receptive	✓								✓			✓	
Reference resources		✓											
Reformulation								✓					
Resources		✓	✓		✓	✓	✓			✓	✓		✓
Rhyme							✓		✓				
Role-play							✓		✓		✓	✓	
Routine	✓				✓		✓			✓			
Rubrics								✓					
Scaffolding								✓					
Scan					✓		✓					✓	
Self-assessment		✓									✓	✓	✓
Self-correction		✓											✓

Term/Unit	1	2	3	4	5	6	7	8	9	10	11	12	13
Settler							✓		✓	✓			
Stage					✓								
Stirrer							✓		✓	✓			
Student talking time (STT)										✓			
Subskill									✓			✓	
Summative (assessment)											✓		
Supplement		✓				✓	✓						
Supplementary materials/resources						✓	✓						
Syllabus		✓			✓	✓	✓				✓		
Syllabus fit					✓								
Target language					✓				✓	✓		✓	
Teacher talking time (TTT)										✓			
TPR (Total Physical Response)	✓						✓	✓	✓				✓
Transcript						✓							
Visualisation	✓							✓					
Wait time			✓					✓					✓
Whole class	✓	✓		✓	✓				✓	✓			✓
Word bank						✓		✓					
Worksheet							✓				✓	✓	✓

Glossary of TKT: Young Learners terms

Term	Definition	Unit(s)
Action song	A song which has actions to accompany it, for example a song about daily routine, where learners listen to and/or sing the song and mime the different routine activities as they hear them, such as get up; brush your teeth, etc.	1
At-home task	An activity or task the learner is asked to do outside of the classroom. Often this is done at home; sometimes call 'homework'. The task should review, consolidate or extend learning, or it might be in preparation for a lesson.	1, 2, 5, 6, 8, 12
Big book	A very large sized storybook or **picturebook**, which is large enough for the teacher to hold, facing towards the learners, as (s)he reads the book with them.	6
Circle time	A phase of the lesson where learners sit in a circle, often on a carpet on the floor. This allows **whole-class activities** and games, allows teacher and learners to have a good view of everyone in the class. It also helps learners feel a sense of belonging to a group (the class).	1, 10
Cross-curricular	A theme, topic, focus or skill which is relevant to, taught in or important for more than one **school subject**, that is it spans different elements of the **curriculum**.	7
Developmental	Adjective: related to the cognitive, physical, social, emotional, linguistic, etc. development of the child	1, 3
Display board	An area on a classroom, corridor or another wall in the school where learners' work, posters and so on can be placed for display. It may be an area of a notice board in or outside of the classroom.	7
Drama activities	In this kind of physical activity, learners mime, perform or pretend. They take on a role of another person, character or animal. It involves a script, which may be provided, improvised or learner-written. It is often to an audience, but may not always be so.	4, 7, 9
Exit ticket	A strategy to informally assess learning in a lesson where a learner completes a mini review task or answers a question at the end of the lesson before they leave. It may be an open question or vary between learners, depending on their learning needs.	5, 7
Extra-curricular	Learning or an activity which is not part of the **curriculum**. It is often optional (for parents or children).	1

Term	Definition	Unit(s)
Fast finisher	A learner who completes an activity or task more quickly than others. It is important to consider these learners when we plan so that we can prepare an activity for them which will extend or enrich their learning and prevent them from disturbing others in the class.	8, 13
Fine motor skills	Bodily movement skills which use the small muscles, usually in the hands or feet. For example, cutting and using scissors, holding a pencil, wiggling your toes.	1
Free play	Play which is completely directed by the child(ren). The children are free to play how they want, with whoever and whatever they like. There is no adult direction or instruction.	8, 9
Gallery walk	An activity which follows the display of learners' work, for example on the classroom noticeboard. Learners walk around freely and look at each other's work. They will ask questions and make comments on it between themselves and with the teacher.	1
Game/game-like activities	Games (and game-like activities) are activities which have a clear purpose, structure, roles and often formulaic scripts. They are usually fun and language learning games often draw on those from other areas of children's lives. See Mourão with Ellis, 2020, Chapter 4 for more on this.	1, 9
Kim's Game	An activity often used to help learn vocabulary. The teacher shows various items (or pictures) on the **IWB**, projector or on a table or tray. Learners close their eyes and the teacher takes away one item. Learners try to remember what was there to say what the teacher took away (and repeat). This cognitive strategy supports memory and attention skills.	7
KWL (Know-Want to know-Learned); KWL chart	In this model, before a topic, lesson or classroom activity, children **brainstorm** what they already **K**now (content and/or language). Then they express what they **W**ant to know, that is they set learning objectives, also in relation to content and/or language. Once the topic, lesson or activity is over, they return to their objectives, reflect and say what they feel they **L**earned. A **KWL chart** is a **worksheet** where learners record their responses at each stage.	2, 12
Language of instruction	The language which is used in the school and in the regular classroom. It may be the children's **L1** or it may be another language. Sometimes it is English, in a non-English-speaking context; also known as EMI (English Medium Instruction)	1

Term	Definition	Unit(s)
Motor skills	Bodily skills of physical movement.	1, 9
Multisensory resources	Resources which stimulate more than one sense at once: sight, hearing, touch, smell, taste. Such resources support different learning preferences and enrich learning.	7
Numeracy	The skills of understanding and working with numbers.	11
Parentese	The modified language that a parent or caregiver uses when they speak to a baby or young child. Among other features, it tends to use repeated, very simple language, is slower, more deliberate, often higher pitched and can sometimes use 'baby talk'. Also known as 'motherese'.	8
Pelmanism	A game played with a set of flashcards which have multiple pairs of cards (two the same, a word and a matching picture, associated words, etc.). All the cards are mixed together and laid out face-down. Learners take turns to turn over two cards and try to find pairs. Various rules can be applied to make this a language-oriented game. It is often used for vocabulary and reading practice, and is a cognitive strategy.	9
Picturebook / Storybook	Books which use a combination of pictures and words to tell a story. These are often designed for very young children, but can also be found in language teaching to children, especially under 8 or 9 years old. A book which tells a story, with more emphasis on the words than the pictures, usually for older children, is a storybook.	1, 6, 7
Playground	An area in a school where children play. It is often outside and may be equipped with slides, climbing frames and so on.	4, 7
Primary	Primary school is often the beginning of compulsory education in many contexts. It is the level of schooling for children aged 5 or 6 to 10 or 11 years old. It is sometimes referred to as Basic Education or Elementary School.	1
Print-rich	An environment which is rich in examples of written language. This may be posters, labels, signs, word cards, word walls, newspaper cuttings and so on. This exposure to written language sensitises learners to written English and supports motivation for learning to read.	7, 10
Puppet	A toy character which can be animated, usually with the hand. Often an animal or person, which can be animated by the teacher or learners so it has a character, it speaks and moves, as it interacts with learners.	7

Term	Definition	Unit(s)
Puzzle	An activity where learners put pieces together to make a whole. It may be a picture, or it could be words. It could also be a problem-solving activity, such as a mystery to solve where learners put pieces of information together to solve the puzzle.	1
School inspectors	Official representatives of an education ministry or governing body who conduct regular visits to schools to monitor and evaluate teaching, learning and other factors to assure quality.	5
Secondary	Secondary school is the next stage of education after Primary or Elementary school. Children may begin around 10 to 12 years old. It is sometimes split between lower and upper, or middle/junior and high school.	1
Storybook	See **picturebook**.	8
(School) subject	Subjects learned in a school context, such as maths, science, languages, geography and so on. These may be taught by a subject teacher, who teaches just that subject, or by a class or generalist teacher, who teaches all the subjects to one class, often integrated in the daily school timetable.	1, 2
Think-Pair-Share	In this strategy, the teacher asks learners to think about and sometimes to note their answer to a question or a task individually first. Then they have time to share their answers or ideas with a partner. Finally, the teacher **nominates** or learners volunteer to share their answers with the class or group. This gives learners time to reflect before answering, supports peer learning and helps them build confidence to contribute to the class.	3, 10
Transition	The moments of a lesson between activities, where one finishes and another starts. Learners may need to stop what they are doing and/or organise their materials and **resources**, and/or move to another area of the classroom or seating arrangement.	1
Webquest	A learning task where learners use the internet to answer a series of questions, mini-tasks or clues, which takes them on a virtual journey around different websites to complete an overall task (the quest).	9
Whole child (development/ approach)	This approach to teaching and learning emphasises the importance of focusing on multiple areas of development. As such, when teaching English, we should also consider how we are helping children develop cognitively, metacognitively, physically, emotionally and so on. We may focus on social skills, learning strategies and content areas (e.g. **CLIL**) as well as English to support development of the whole child.	7, 9

Test tips for TKT: Young Learners

The TKT: YL Module test has 80 questions and lasts for 80 minutes. The questions are all closed, single-answer questions, which are recorded on an answer sheet (see the sample on page 184). They are a combination of multiple choice, matching, ordering and identifying the odd one out.

Preparing for the test.
To help prepare for the test, you are strongly recommended to:
✓ work through the units in this book, including reading the unit content and doing the pre-reading, follow-up and discovery tasks, which will introduce you to key terminology, deepen your understanding of key concepts and help you connect your learning to teaching practice.
✓ Review the list of TKT: YL terms used in this book and in the *TKT Glossary* online. Make sure that you understand these terms: reflect on the concepts behind them and their application to teaching and learning.
✓ Do timed TKT: YL practice tests. You will find sample questions at the end of each unit in this book as well as a complete sample test. You will also find a complete sample TKT: YL test on the Cambridge Assessment website.
✓ Review your answers to sample test material and reflect on any mistakes you made. Review the relevant unit(s) in this book as necessary.

During the test.
✓ Open your question booklet when you are told to do so and briefly look through the whole paper to get an idea of its content.
✓ Work through the test questions in order. Mark your answer directly on the answer sheet as you do this or you could note them on the booklet to transfer later to the answer sheet. If you do this, you will need to have plenty of time to do this carefully and accurately.
✓ Remember to use a pencil, not a pen. If you rub out any answers to change them, make sure you do this carefully so there are no pencil marks on the incorrect answer spaces.
✓ Always read the instructions for the questions carefully **before** attempting to answer them. Make sure you understand what is being presented (e.g. teachers' or learners' comments, or a lesson plan extract) and what you are being asked to do.
✓ Take care with odd-one-out questions, which ask about what is NOT true or correct.
✓ Take care with matching questions as some may have more options to match than questions, so some will not be used.
✓ Don't spend too long on one question. If you are unsure of an answer, you could put the answer you think is correct on the answer sheet, and circle the question on your question booklet. Then you can return to it later, if you have time, when you have completed the 80 questions.
✓ Avoid second-guessing the answer key (e.g. if I've used answers A and B already, then it must be C). This is not a useful strategy and could take up a lot of your time and mental energy.
✓ Give yourself at least five minutes to carefully transfer your answers, as needed, and check them carefully. The invigilator will let you know when you have ten minutes left.
✓ Try to relax. If you feel nervous or stressed, pause, close your eyes and take a deep breath to help you refocus. Do the best you can, but you don't need to aim for perfection!

TEACHING KNOWLEDGE TEST
YOUNG LEARNERS

Practice Test

1 hour 20 minutes

INSTRUCTIONS TO CANDIDATES

Do not open this question paper until you are told to do so.

Write your name, centre number and candidate number on your answer sheet if they are not already there.

Read the instructions for each part of the paper carefully.

Answer all the questions.

Read the instructions on the answer sheet.

Mark your answers on the answer sheet. Use a pencil.

You **must** complete the answer sheet within the time limit.

At the end of the test, hand in both this question paper and your answer sheet.

INFORMATION FOR CANDIDATES

There are 80 questions in this paper.

Each question carries one mark.

PV1
© Cambridge University Press & Assessment 2023

For questions **1–7**, match the strategies teachers aim to develop with the instructions listed **A–C**. Mark the correct letter (**A–C**) on your answer sheet.

Teachers' instructions

A	only instruction X
B	only instruction Y
C	both instructions X and Y

Strategies teachers aim to develop

1 The teacher wants the children to categorise lexis.

Instruction X: Look at the words on the cards and put them into piles of animal words, clothes words and people words.

Instruction Y: I'm going to say some words. Put your hand up each time you know a word I say.

2 The teacher wants the children to develop predicting skills.

Instruction X: Tell me six things that you <u>know</u> you are going to do tomorrow.

Instruction Y: I'm going to tell you a story called *The Princess and the Frog*. What do you think the story will be about?

3 The teacher wants the children to learn how to scan a text.

Instruction X: Underline all the names of people in this little story.

Instruction Y: Draw a picture which shows the main thing that happens in the story.

4 The teacher wants the children to develop fluency by doing a ranking exercise.

Instruction X: With a partner, number these seven birthday presents. Number 1 is the present you would most like most; number 2 the second most and so on.

Instruction Y: Please put yourselves in a line, with the smallest person at the front and the tallest at the back.

5 The teacher wants to see how good the children are at deducing the meaning of vocabulary from context.

Instruction X: Look at the text. Highlight all the uses of *he*, *she* and *it*.

Instruction Y: Look at these sentences from the text with words underlined. Can you give a definition of the words?

6 The teacher wants the children to work on sequencing when telling a story.

Instruction X: On each piece of paper you have one sentence from a fairy tale. Put them together to make the story.

Instruction Y: These pictures show some children having an adventure. Can you use them to tell a story?

7 The teacher wants to improve the children's confidence in risk-taking.

Instruction X: Tell me about yourself and your family. If you make a mistake, just carry on.

The important thing is to practice speaking.

Instruction Y: These pictures show some children having an adventure. Can you use them to tell a story?

For questions **8–13**, look at the statements about supporting children's characteristics as language learners and choose the option (**A**, **B** or **C**) which does **NOT** complete each statement.

Mark the letter (**A**, **B** or **C**) which does **NOT** complete each statement correctly on your answer sheet.

---

8 Praising good behaviour and commenting on good work establishes positive relationships with children, so I

- **A**   encourage children to think carefully before doing a difficult task.
- **B**   give stars to pairs and groups who work well together.
- **C**   use words like *great*, *well done* and *good work* all the time.

9 Using language chunks is an important part of language learning for children, so I

- **A**   use jazz chants to build children's confidence with language.
- **B**   use substitution tables to practise target language.
- **C**   use word cards to raise awareness of individual lexical items.

10 Some children have a limited attention span, so I

- **A**   vary interaction patterns and task types.
- **B**   include both stir and settle activities in my lessons.
- **C**   provide regular opportunities for extensive listening.

11 Developing literacy is a key part of children's learning, so I

- **A**   ask the class to tell their personal stories after the weekend or holidays.
- **B**   use storybook reading as a whole class activity or for individual fast finishers.
- **C**   often ask children to write letters, words or sentences on the board.

12 The children I teach may be at different stages of cognitive development, so I

- **A**   plan tasks which involve both concrete and abstract thinking.
- **B**   provide extra challenge for children who need it.
- **C**   concentrate on tasks which involve children doing practical activities with real objects.

13 Children respond positively to familiar routines in the classroom, so I

- **A**   start by taking the register and finish by reviewing lesson language.
- **B**   use different seating plans during the term.
- **C**   set clear rules of classroom behaviour.

For questions **14–20**, match the extracts from a lesson plan in which children draw and write about pictures of monsters with the lesson plan headings listed **A–H**.

Mark the correct letter (**A–H**) on your answer sheet.

There is one extra option which you do not need to use.

Lesson plan headings

A	Assessment of learning
B	Interaction patterns
C	Personal teaching aim
D	Follow-up suggestions
E	Learning outcomes
F	Resources
G	Differentiation
H	Previous learning

Extracts from a lesson plan

14 Whole class; group; pairs; individual

15 Children know colours, body parts and has/have got.

16 Pictures of three different monsters, colouring pens and pencils, worksheets 1 and 2, plain paper

17 Give children a questionnaire to complete with smiley faces for their learning diaries.

18 Production of a picture of a monster with short descriptive text

19 Remember not to interrupt children when they are speaking.

20 Invite another class to read or hear the descriptions and try to identify the appropriate monster.

For questions **21–26**, match the problems teachers have with using films in class with possible solutions for providing support listed **A–G**.

Mark the correct letter (**A–G**) on your answer sheet.

There is one extra option which you do not need to use.

Teachers' problems		Possible solutions for providing support
21	Some films have a lot of different characters in them.	**A** Work in pairs or small groups.
22	Some children complain that they've seen a film before and I don't want them to be bored.	**B** Stop the film and ask children to predict the next scene.
23	There is no opportunity for speaking practice while watching the film.	**C** Establish clear behaviour rules before watching a film.
24	Children are often unable to sit still for very long.	**D** Show the film in parts over a series of lessons.
25	Some films contain a number of words that are beyond the children's level.	**E** Give children a handout with pictures and names.
26	Some children are likely to speak and disturb others during the film.	**F** Provide challenge by using worksheets which include extension activities.
		G Prepare target vocabulary lists to study before watching.

For questions **27–34**, look at the advice about preparing storybook-based material for children and choose the option (**A–C**) which completes each statement.

Mark the correct letter (**A–C**) on your answer sheet.

---

27 Identify language and learning goals which correspond to the story by
    A   making reference to schemes of work and course syllabuses.
    B   checking results of peer and self-assessment tasks.
    C   asking the class what types of stories they like and dislike.

28 Choose a story and, wherever necessary, adapt difficult language by
    A   using L1 to narrate parts of the story.
    B   simplifying the verb tenses and descriptive vocabulary.
    C   describing only what children can see in the illustrations.

29 Decide what additional materials to prepare for the story such as
    A   sentence transformation tasks.
    B   'Can-do' statements.
    C   domino games in which children sequence sentences.

30 Make the story relevant to the class by
    A   connecting the story to their own experience in some way.
    B   allowing them to read the story alone beforehand.
    C   selecting a story with a surprising ending.

31 Plan how to manage the classroom so everyone has a good view of the book and teacher by
    A   arranging to use the school hall or other large area.
    B   asking the class to sit on the floor in a semi-circle in front of you.
    C   removing from the classroom walls visual aids which may attract children's attention.

32 Select storytelling techniques which best suit the story and target language such as
    A   using mime to focus on target language.
    B   asking children to take it in turns to read pages of the storybook aloud.
    C   asking children to proofread the story.

33 Prepare review ideas for the story by including
    A   displays of children's work related to the story.
    B   continuous assessment tasks.
    C   games which focus on action words.

34 Assess the language and learning outcomes of story-based work by
    A   using a placement test.
    B   using a transcript.
    C   using a checklist.

For questions **35–40**, look at the scaffolding provided in different coursebook activities and the three descriptions of this scaffolding (**A–C**).

Choose the description which matches the scaffolding used in the coursebook.

Mark the correct letter (**A–C**) on your answer sheet.

---

35 Use this example to help you talk about the picture.

The boy		an ice-cream.
The girl		a sandwich.
The baby	is eating	an apple.
The man		an orange.
The woman		a banana.

A   providing a word bank
B   providing a glossary
C   providing a substitution table

36 Use this example to help you write your letter.

Dear _____

Are you free on _____ ?

I'm going to the _____ . Would you like to come _____ ?

Your friend,

_____

A   providing a sentence starter
B   providing a language frame
C   providing a speech bubble

37 Help the farmer to count his animals!

A   providing a clear purpose for an activity
B   providing a language model
C   providing a demonstration

38 Ask three friends about their favourite food.

Friend	Favourite food

A   using realia
B   using a multisensory activity
C   using personal experiences to relate to learning content

39 Use this example to talk about how our class gets to school.

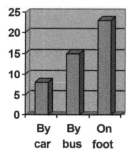

A   using a bar chart
B   using a pie chart
C   using a flow chart

40 Say the names of three things in this bedroom.

A   encouraging children to predict
B   encouraging children to record lexis
C   encouraging children to use context

For questions **41–47**, match what the teacher says with the scaffolding strategies listed **A–H**.

Mark the correct letter (**A–H**) on your answer sheet.

There is one extra option which you do not need to use.

Scaffolding strategies

A	creating a familiar context for an activity
B	supporting meaning with visual realia
C	connecting meaning with physical activity
D	providing a meaningful purpose for an activity
E	demonstrating how to do an activity
F	checking understanding of meaning through a concept question
G	providing a language model for an activity
H	using a chart to help children consolidate learning

What the teacher says

41 Now stand up and do what I say – but only if I say Simon says before my instructions. Is that clear?

42 Watch while Jose and I play the card game. Then you can try it yourselves.

43 Some other classes are going to come and watch the short plays you have prepared. So you must speak very clearly.

44 Write the animals with an /æ/ sound in their name in the first column, animals with an /ɪ/ sound in the second column and animals with an /ɒ/ sound in the third column.

45 Use the example holiday postcard I've written on the board to help you write a card to your English friend.

46 You like to watch television, don't you? Your favourite programme has just begun and your mum says you must go and do your homework at once. What do you say to her?

47 If you are looking forward to seeing someone, do you want to see them or not?

For questions **48–54**, match the teachers' reasons for using different activities in the young learner classroom with the practice activities listed **A–H**.

Mark the correct letter (**A–H**) on your answer sheet.

There is one extra option which you do not need to use.

Practice activities

A	problem solving
B	songs
C	listen and do
D	role-play
E	brainstorming
F	dictation
G	surveys
H	writing stories

Teachers' reasons for using different activities

48 Children enjoy moving around, talking to each other to get information and having a task to complete. Using these activities is a powerful way of developing questioning skills. Other skills are also practised as the answers to questions have to be recognised and recorded.

49 These activities energise children. If done orally in open class, they can be fast moving and can give children language and ideas for following activities.

50 Children enjoy doing this type of activity – it allows them to use their natural ability to mimic and encourages them to communicate about things that they might not talk about usually.

51 These activities help children to learn language with ease. For example, chunks of language and word and sentence stress are supported and made memorable.

52 Children love activities like these which get them moving. They don't need to understand everything – just the instructions. They give them the chance to acquire the language.

53 These activities are enjoyable and allow children to share their feelings. Children practise language in context and can support their work with pictures.

54 Children need to work through a number of steps to find the right answer in a task. These activities can also support cognitive development.

For questions **55–61**, look at the statements about the uses of classroom practice activities and choose the option (**A, B** or **C**) which does **NOT** complete each statement.

Mark the correct letter (**A, B** or **C**) which does **NOT** complete each statement correctly on your answer sheet.

---

55 Stirring activities can be used to

    A   create a competitive atmosphere in the classroom.

    B   provide children with practice of language in pairs and groups.

    C   calm and quieten children after a game or an active task.

56 Chants can be used to focus on

    A   language chunks.

    B   creative writing.

    C   pronunciation.

57 Class surveys provide an opportunity for children to

    A   review on their own in the class.

    B   interview a partner in the class.

    C   mingle with others in the class.

58 Brainstorming ideas provides an opportunity for children to

    A   revise language learnt previously.

    B   develop their ability to talk about their own experience.

    C   guess meaning from context.

59 Information-gap activities can be used to help children to

    A   focus on word boundaries.

    B   learn from social interaction.

    C   remember language and content.

60 Dictation activities can help children to focus on

    A   punctuation.

    B   spelling.

    C   linking.

61 Songs can be used with children to

    A   establish routines so that children feel comfortable.

    B   develop awareness of layout.

    C   develop children's ability to listen for gist and detail.

For questions **62–67**, match the problems teachers have identified from observing classes with the classroom management solutions listed **A–G**.

Mark the correct letter (**A–G**) on your answer sheet. There is one extra option which you do not need to use.

Classroom management solutions

A	Have your own supply which you collect again at the end of the lesson.
B	Introduce children to a puppet who does not know the children's L1.
C	Ask children to repeat your instructions in L1.
D	Speak together in L1 after the class if you think this is necessary.
E	Use more settlers in your lesson.
F	Use pictures and oral drills to clarify.
G	Use short activities and vary interaction patterns.

Problems identified during classroom observation

62 Children are not sure how to say the time in English.

63 Some children often forget to bring pencils or pens to lessons.

64 Some children are very tired in the last lesson of the day.

65 A child seems very upset at the end of a lesson.

66 Children sometimes get overexcited if there are a lot of games in class.

67 Some children seem a little shy to speak English.

For questions **68–73**, match the classroom tasks with the main reasons for assessing learning listed **A**, **B** and **C**.

Mark the correct letter (**A**, **B** or **C**) on your answer sheet.

Main reasons for assessing learning

A	identifying achievement in learning vocabulary
B	identifying strengths and weaknesses in organising learning
C	identifying whether the children can narrate past events

Classroom tasks

68 Children work in groups to plan their end-of-term presentations and agree responsibilities.

69 Children write about what they did on the trip to the local history museum last week.

70 Children look at a picture of a day on the beach and read a text. They have to circle things they can see in the picture that the text mentions.

71 Children match the names of the ingredients of a cake they tasted yesterday with their definitions.

72 Children decide and note down what their group project will be on and where they are going to look for information they want to include.

73 Children work in pairs and tell each other three things that they did at the weekend. They then report this back to the class.

For questions **74–80**, read the teachers' comments about acting on assessment evidence. Match Teacher Y's comments with the appropriate classroom action listed **A–D**.

Mark the correct letter (**A–D**) on your answer sheet.

Classroom action following assessment

A	provide written formative feedback
B	select practice activities to review and clarify areas of learning
C	adjust areas of classroom management
D	modify task types

Teachers' comments

74 **Teacher X:** Lots of children in my class are unclear about word order.
Teacher Y: Why don't you prepare a class survey to focus on question forms?

75 **Teacher X:** I'm finding it very difficult to get the class to finish tasks. The children want to go on forever!
Teacher Y: Have you tried setting a time limit for the task and then counting down towards the end?

76 **Teacher X:** That listening exercise didn't work. It was much too complicated for children to listen, read the class timetable and fill in the gaps at the same time.
Teacher Y: I've had the same problem. Reducing the number of gaps seems to help.

77 **Teacher X:** The children's work isn't improving as quickly as I'd hoped.
Teacher Y: I usually give a grade or mark on homework with a suggestion of one thing to work on such as spelling or organisation for next time.

78 **Teacher X:** I noticed that some children found it very hard to assess their partner's work for the peer-assessment task.
Teacher Y: Well, next time why don't you give a demonstration before the task, or ask some volunteers to give their assessments as examples?

79 **Teacher X:** The children seemed to really enjoy speaking to me individually in the oral test but they were sometimes distracted by the behaviour of their classmates.
Teacher Y: What about arranging the interview so the child has their back to the class, so that you can still monitor what's going on?

80 **Teacher X:** The vocabulary and spelling was good in the story-writing task but they need to work on continuity and joining sentences together.
Teacher Y: You could try using a sentence dominoes game.

Sample test answer sheet for TKT: YL practice test

CAMBRIDGE English

Candidate Name		Candidate Number	
Centre Name		Centre Number	
Examination Title		Examination Details	
Candidate Signature		Assessment Date	

Supervisor: If the candidate is ABSENT or has WITHDRAWN shade here ○

Teaching Knowledge Test Candidate Answer Sheet

Instructions
Use a PENCIL (B or HB).
Rub out any answer you want to change with an eraser.

For Parts 1, 2, 3, 4 and 5:
Mark ONE letter for each answer.
For example: If you think A is the right answer to the question, mark your answer sheet like this:

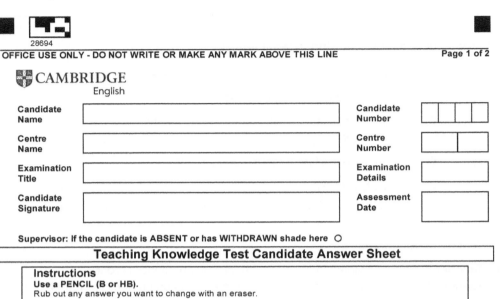

1 A B C D E F G H I
2 A B C D E F G H I
3 A B C D E F G H I
4 A B C D E F G H I
5 A B C D E F G H I
6 A B C D E F G H I
7 A B C D E F G H I
8 A B C D E F G H I
9 A B C D E F G H I
10 A B C D E F G H I
11 A B C D E F G H I
12 A B C D E F G H I

13 A B C D E F G H I
14 A B C D E F G H I
15 A B C D E F G H I
16 A B C D E F G H I
17 A B C D E F G H I
18 A B C D E F G H I
19 A B C D E F G H I
20 A B C D E F G H I
21 A B C D E F G H I
22 A B C D E F G H I
23 A B C D E F G H I
24 A B C D E F G H I

Sample test answer sheet for TKT: YL practice test

28694

OFFICE USE ONLY - DO NOT WRITE OR MAKE ANY MARK ABOVE THIS LINE Page 2 of 2

#	A	B	C	D	E	F	G	H	I
25	○	○	○	○	○	○	○	○	○
26	○	○	○	○	○	○	○	○	○
27	○	○	○	○	○	○	○	○	○
28	○	○	○	○	○	○	○	○	○
29	○	○	○	○	○	○	○	○	○
30	○	○	○	○	○	○	○	○	○
31	○	○	○	○	○	○	○	○	○
32	○	○	○	○	○	○	○	○	○
33	○	○	○	○	○	○	○	○	○
34	○	○	○	○	○	○	○	○	○
35	○	○	○	○	○	○	○	○	○
36	○	○	○	○	○	○	○	○	○
37	○	○	○	○	○	○	○	○	○
38	○	○	○	○	○	○	○	○	○
39	○	○	○	○	○	○	○	○	○
40	○	○	○	○	○	○	○	○	○
41	○	○	○	○	○	○	○	○	○
42	○	○	○	○	○	○	○	○	○
43	○	○	○	○	○	○	○	○	○
44	○	○	○	○	○	○	○	○	○
45	○	○	○	○	○	○	○	○	○
46	○	○	○	○	○	○	○	○	○
47	○	○	○	○	○	○	○	○	○
48	○	○	○	○	○	○	○	○	○
49	○	○	○	○	○	○	○	○	○
50	○	○	○	○	○	○	○	○	○
51	○	○	○	○	○	○	○	○	○
52	○	○	○	○	○	○	○	○	○

#	A	B	C	D	E	F	G	H	I
53	○	○	○	○	○	○	○	○	○
54	○	○	○	○	○	○	○	○	○
55	○	○	○	○	○	○	○	○	○
56	○	○	○	○	○	○	○	○	○
57	○	○	○	○	○	○	○	○	○
58	○	○	○	○	○	○	○	○	○
59	○	○	○	○	○	○	○	○	○
60	○	○	○	○	○	○	○	○	○
61	○	○	○	○	○	○	○	○	○
62	○	○	○	○	○	○	○	○	○
63	○	○	○	○	○	○	○	○	○
64	○	○	○	○	○	○	○	○	○
65	○	○	○	○	○	○	○	○	○
66	○	○	○	○	○	○	○	○	○
67	○	○	○	○	○	○	○	○	○
68	○	○	○	○	○	○	○	○	○
69	○	○	○	○	○	○	○	○	○
70	○	○	○	○	○	○	○	○	○
71	○	○	○	○	○	○	○	○	○
72	○	○	○	○	○	○	○	○	○
73	○	○	○	○	○	○	○	○	○
74	○	○	○	○	○	○	○	○	○
75	○	○	○	○	○	○	○	○	○
76	○	○	○	○	○	○	○	○	○
77	○	○	○	○	○	○	○	○	○
78	○	○	○	○	○	○	○	○	○
79	○	○	○	○	○	○	○	○	○
80	○	○	○	○	○	○	○	○	○

OFFICE USE ONLY - DO NOT WRITE OR MAKE ANY MARK BELOW THIS LINE Page 2 of 2

28694

185

Answer key for TKT: YL practice test

1	A	41	C
2	B	42	E
3	A	43	D
4	A	44	H
5	B	45	G
6	C	46	A
7	C	47	F
8	A	48	G
9	C	49	E
10	C	50	D
11	A	51	B
12	C	52	C
13	B	53	H
14	B	54	A
15	H	55	C
16	F	56	B
17	A	57	A
18	E	58	C
19	C	59	A
20	D	60	C
21	E	61	B
22	F	62	F
23	B	63	A
24	D	64	G
25	G	65	D
26	C	66	E
27	A	67	B
28	B	68	B
29	C	69	C
30	A	70	A
31	B	71	A
32	A	72	B
33	A	73	C
34	C	74	B
35	C	75	C
36	B	76	D
37	A	77	A
38	C	78	C
39	A	79	C
40	C	80	B